The Charmed Life
MASTER PLANNER
2019

Created by Alexis C Giostra

Published by Charmed Media Enterprises, LLC
www.StrangeCharmed.com

CREATING YOUR MASTER PLAN

The Charmed Life Master Planner is broken into three distinct sections, giving you dedicated spaces to manage your time, track projects and come up with all your brilliant ideas for the year!

The Functional Planning Philosophy
Pages 5-9

The Charmed Life Master Planner begins with a few brief worksheets and tip sheets that outline the basic productivity philosophy behind functional planning. Functional planning is a holistic method of planning designed to help you focus on your priorities and the projects and tasks associated with them, so you are spending your time intentionally creating the life you want to live.

Manage Your Time
Pages 10-171

The majority of The Charmed Life Master Planner is the 12 month dated calendar that contains the following:

- Year at a Glance Calendar, Yearly Tracker & Yearly Overview for reference and long term planning for the full year.
- *Month on Two Pages:* Each month begins with a month on two pages spread giving you an overview of your month and important dates or events on your calendar.
- *Master Monthly Task Page:* Identify the tasks you need to accomplish for the month and keep them organized here.
- *Monthly Tracker Sheet:* Keep track of reoccuring or scheduled actions for the month.
- *Week on Two Pages:* Identify your top 3 tasks each day and priorities them at the top of your list with room to spare for additional tasks, schedule info, or notes.

Track Projects
Pages 172-255

The second section of The Charmed Life Master Planner is Important Projects. This section begins with a yearly project matrix where you can map out your short, mid and long term projects for each month, quarter and half of the year.

Next, you can break each project out in detail and track the progress of tasks on the two page project plan with notes. Project planning is an essential part of the functional planning process to help you make important objectives for your life and work a reality.

Create Your Brilliant Ideas
Pages 256-375

The final section of The Charmed Life Master Planner is dedicated to creating your Brilliant Ideas and is so much more than the standard note section of a planner! The section begins with Braindump sheets where you can list out all the important and random ideas, information and tasks you have been storing in your brain and get them all out on paper. I recommend performing a brain dump at least once a month to keep your mind clear and focused on processing information, as opposed to storing information (you've got your planner for that)! Once you've got all your ideas out of your head, you can begin to prioritize them on the second page that includes a Time Management Grid based on the design by Stephen Covey in *The 7 Habits of Highly Effective People*. List the tasks from your brain dump out into the proper quadrant based on their importance and urgency to determine how you will prioritize items for their completion. Don't forget! Just because an item is listed on this grid doesn't mean YOU need to be the one to complete the task. Delegation is also a key factor in time management, so make sure you absolutely need to be the one to complete a task, even the most important and urgent ones!

The next sheets in this section are Brainstorm sheets to help you generate and organize ideas. Use the grid of squares to lay out a potential project or objective and use the individual squares to outline categories, groups of tasks or individual elements of the project until you have your ideas out and ready to be turned into a project plan!

Of course, this section also includes a number of extra blank note pages for you to create additional lists or details for anything in your life.

The final pages of the planner are a blank Index where you can keep track of the ideas and contents of the pages of the planner for quick reference and organization. Feel free to list all the pages of the planner and their contents or create groups of topics and keep them listed out together for quick reference.

Need More Planner Inspiration & Ideas?

The Charmed Life Master Planner was designed to be a functional and flexible tool for you to create the Master Plan for your year and life, so if you want more brilliant ideas for how to use the planner you will find articles, video how-to's and more at: **www.YourMasterPlanner.com**

PART 1: IDENTIFYING YOUR PRIORITIES

The first step to functional planning is to understand and acknowledge your individual priorities. Priorities are elements or areas of your life that you deem more important than others. We choose our priorities based on our own values and life situations, but this process is essential in order to achieve a sense of harmony and a feeling that we are in control of our lives. By identifying 3-5 areas of our lives as priorities and ranking them by importance, we are better able to manage our time around what is important to us.

In the space below, I want you to identify 3-5 priorities and list them by highest priority first!

My Priorities

_____

_____

_____

_____

_____

Now I want you to take each of your priorities and define 1-3 specific tasks you will take on a regular basis to ensure you are prioritizing this element of your life. For example, if one of your priorities was your family, you may list a weekly family dinner or game night as a non negotiable task that you will make room for in your schedule in order to ensure you are nurturing your family as a priority.

	Task	Freq.
Priority #1: _____	_____	_____
	Task	Freq.
Priority #2: _____	_____	_____
	Task	Freq.
Priority #3 _____	_____	_____
	Task	Freq.
Priority #4: _____	_____	_____
	Task	Freq.
Priority #5: _____	_____	_____

PART 2: ESTABLISHING ROUTINES

The second step to functional planning is to establish routines to support successful execution of time management and tasks. Routines are organized sequences of fixed actions that are executed regularly or at a specific frequency. Individuals can build routines for any aspect of their life that they regularly execute on, for example an exercise routine or a study routine. Most routines will vary by individual preference, however, there are two types of routines that have been shown to yield great results in terms of personal productivity; the morning routine and the evening routine. Essentially, these routines are a sequence of tasks that an individual will perform upon waking and at the close of the day in order to wind down for sleep. The exact tasks that an individual will perform during their morning and evening routines may vary, however, studies have shown that including a few specific tasks can increase daily productivity by at least 30%. In the space provided below, define your own individual morning and evening routines by adding your specific daily tasks to the list of suggested actions for optimum productivity!

Morning Routine	*Evening Routine*
o Wake Up	o Change into comfortable clothing
o Make bed	o Drink a glass of water before bed
o Drink a glass of water	o Turn off gadgets within an hour of sleep
o Stretch and/or meditate for 15-30 mins	o Engage in a relaxing activity like reading
o Ignore gadgets for 30 minutes upon waking	o Don't eat anything within 3-4 hours of sleep
o	o
o	o
o	o
o	o
o	o

PART 3: BUILDING POSITIVE HABITS

Aristotle once said "*We are what we repeatedly do. Excellent therefore is not an act, but a habit.*" If the sum achievement of our lives can be defined by our daily habits alone, it's essential that we strive to build positive habits into our lives and dispose of any negative or harmful habits. If you have ever tried to get rid of a bad habit before, you probably already know that it's not as easy as it seems, so here are some tips for building positive habits and replacing negative ones.

Tip #1: *Swap a bad habit for a* *good habit*	*Tip #2:* *Identify a cue to build a* *new positive habit*	*Tip #3:* *Track your* *progress*

Habits, like routines, are not easily broken, however, if we consciously swap one activity with another, it's possible to keep up positive momentum and fully integrate a new habit into our lives. For example, if you are someone who is trying to break a smoking habit and everyday at a specific time you go out for a cigarette, you can start to replace that habit by choosing to perform another activity at the same time. You could go get coffee, or take a quick walk, something to fill the void so that you are not missing that sense of activity that the smoking break represented.

Sometimes in order to build a new habit, we must identify opportunities to insert a task into our routine. If you are someone, who for instance, is looking to add exercise to your daily routine, you may need to figure out a cue or signal that you can use to re-mind yourself to go work out. If you currently come home from work and head straight to the fridge to get a snack, you may need to use the cue of returning home from work as a signal to change into your workout gear instead of getting that snack. Leave a note on the fridge if it helps you to remember that you are changing your daily habit to integrate that workout, but use that cue of returning home from work as your sign that it's time to get your workout in. Obviously, you need to identify the cue or signal you will use to remind you to perform your new daily habit, but defining your cue will help you build the new habit into your existing routine.

When it comes down to being successful with building new routines and habits, it's very true that you achieve what you measure. If you are not keeping track and measuring your success, you will most likely forget about it. Defining your routines and identifying the habits you want to change is important, but you must measure your success to see the follow through. I have included a *monthly*Tracker for you to use each month to track and measure your success with developing new routines and positive habits. Don't forget to also use your *weekly*Plan to write down and track your success with habits that you are looking to build into your life.

Your time each day is extremely precious, so it's important that you implement functional planning techniques as you determine your plan of action each day. In functional planning there are three key roles your planner must play and if you plan based on these three elements, you will have greater control over your time.

Role #1: Schedule your time

First and foremost, your planner must be used to schedule out your time. Keeping track of appointments, blocking out times for key priority items and marking down reoccurring events or special days.

Role #2: Track your tasks

In order to keep you on track with your priorities and goals, you should keep your tasks listed out in your planner. You can break down your major tasks into project plans and then keep track of your to-dos on a monthly master task list. Referring back to this master list on a daily basis and assigning tasks to specific days or times will help keep you accountable for making progress.

Role #3: Plan your daily actions

Each day should start with a period of reflection on the tasks and scheduled events you will engage in. At the start of each week, determine the five projects that will have your attention for the week and then each day, first thing, set your top three most important actions. Review your schedule for appointments that will take up your time, and then fill in the rest of your day with subsequent actions that should be completed in order of greatest priority.

PART 5: TAKING ACTION

The hardest part of productivity is often taking action on our plans, but once you have a solid plan laid out, you can quickly begin to take action and start a pattern of positive momentum. Nothing is more empowering to our own productivity than taking action and seeing our own progress. Here are some strategies for starting that positive momentum when you lack inspiration to take action.

Tip #1: Make your bed first thing each day

Starting your day with a simple and quick action like making your bed can be a powerful ripple that can be felt for the rest of the day. When you wake up, exit bed immediately and make your bed so that you resist the urge to return to it and feel the positive flow of productivity as you start your morning.

Tip #2: Do the most important tasks first

No matter how productive you are, there will always be items on your daily to do list that you will not accomplish. This is to be expected, so make sure you take care of the most important items for the day as soon as possible. That way, if you get side-tracked or something unexpected halts your productivity, at least your priorities have been met for the day. I firmly believe that when we take care of the most important priorities first, no matter how much we do or do not get done beyond those items, everything else will fall into place.

Tip #3: Bribe yourself

If getting started and taking action on your plans is hard for you, it may be important for your to bribe yourself. Set a reward for yourself if you accomplish your priorities for the day. Eventually, through practice, you will gain a sense of self-confidence that will become its own reward and you will not need to bribe yourself any longer.

Tip #4: Set a timer

For some of us, the pressure of a deadline stirs us to action. So if you are finding it hard to get tasks accomplished, try setting a timer and challenging yourself to complete your action in the determined time.

Tip #5: Just take action

Although it may be hard for us, sometimes the only way we can make progress is to take responsibility for our actions and execute. A body in motion tends to stay in motion, and similarly an individual taking action tends to continue acting. Set aside all your thoughts and fears and get started now!

Time to get started!

*yearly*CALENDAR

twenty

JANUARY

S	M	T	W	T	F	S
		1	2	3	4	5
6	7	8	9	10	11	12
13	14	15	16	17	18	19
20	21	22	23	24	25	26
27	28	29	30	31		

FEBRUARY

S	M	T	W	T	F	S
					1	2
3	4	5	6	7	8	9
10	11	12	13	14	15	16
17	18	19	20	21	22	23
24	25	26	27	28		

MAY

S	M	T	W	T	F	S
			1	2	3	4
5	6	7	8	9	10	11
12	13	14	15	16	17	18
19	20	21	22	23	24	25
26	27	28	29	30	31	

JUNE

S	M	T	W	T	F	S
						1
2	3	4	5	6	7	8
9	10	11	12	13	14	15
16	17	18	19	20	21	22
23	24	25	26	27	28	29
30						

SEPTEMBER

S	M	T	W	T	F	S
1	2	3	4	5	6	7
8	9	10	11	12	13	14
15	16	17	18	19	20	21
22	23	24	25	26	27	28
29	30					

OCTOBER

S	M	T	W	T	F	S
		1	2	3	4	5
6	7	8	9	10	11	12
13	14	15	16	17	18	19
20	21	22	23	24	25	26
27	28	29	30	31		

nineteen

MARCH

S	M	T	W	T	F	S
					1	2
3	4	5	6	7	8	9
10	11	12	13	14	15	16
17	18	19	20	21	22	23
24	25	26	27	28	29	30
31						

APRIL

S	M	T	W	T	F	S
	1	2	3	4	5	6
7	8	9	10	11	12	13
14	15	16	17	18	19	20
21	22	23	24	25	26	27
28	29	30				

JULY

S	M	T	W	T	F	S
	1	2	3	4	5	6
7	8	9	10	11	12	13
14	15	16	17	18	19	20
21	22	23	24	25	26	27
28	29	30	31			

AUGUST

S	M	T	W	T	F	S
				1	2	3
4	5	6	7	8	9	10
11	12	13	14	15	16	17
18	19	20	21	22	23	24
25	26	27	28	29	30	31

NOVEMBER

S	M	T	W	T	F	S
					1	2
3	4	5	6	7	8	9
10	11	12	13	14	15	16
17	18	19	20	21	22	23
24	25	26	27	28	29	30

DECEMBER

S	M	T	W	T	F	S
1	2	3	4	5	6	7
8	9	10	11	12	13	14
15	16	17	18	19	20	21
22	23	24	25	26	27	28
29	30	31				

*yearly*TRACKER

2019	W	T	F	S	S	M	T	W	T	F	S	S	M	T	W	T	F
JANUARY							1	2	3	4	5	6	7	8	9	10	11
FEBRUARY			1	2	3	4	5	6	7	8	9	10	11	12	13	14	15
MARCH			1	2	3	4	5	6	7	8	9	10	11	12	13	14	15
APRIL						1	2	3	4	5	6	7	8	9	10	11	12
MAY	1	2	3	4	5	6	7	8	9	10	11	12	13	14	15	16	17
JUNE				1	2	3	4	5	6	7	8	9	10	11	12	13	14
JULY						1	2	3	4	5	6	7	8	9	10	11	12
AUGUST		1	2	3	4	5	6	7	8	9	10	11	12	13	14	15	16
SEPTEMBER					1	2	3	4	5	6	7	8	9	10	11	12	13
OCTOBER							1	2	3	4	5	6	7	8	9	10	11
NOVEMBER			1	2	3	4	5	6	7	8	9	10	11	12	13	14	15
DECEMBER					1	2	3	4	5	6	7	8	9	10	11	12	13

S	S	M	T	W	T	F	S	S	M	T	W	T	F	S	S	M	T	W	T
12	13	14	15	16	17	18	19	20	21	22	23	24	25	26	27	28	29	30	31
16	17	18	19	20	21	22	23	24	25	26	27	28							
16	17	18	19	20	21	22	23	24	25	26	27	28	29	30	31				
13	14	15	16	17	18	19	20	21	22	23	24	25	26	27	28	29	30		
18	19	20	21	22	23	24	25	26	27	28	29	30	31						
15	16	17	18	19	20	21	22	23	24	25	26	27	28	29	30				
13	14	15	16	17	18	19	20	21	22	23	24	25	26	27	28	29	30	31	
17	18	19	20	21	22	23	24	25	26	27	28	29	30	31					
14	15	16	17	18	19	20	21	22	23	24	25	26	27	28	29	30			
12	13	14	15	16	17	18	19	20	21	22	23	24	25	26	27	28	29	30	31
16	17	18	19	20	21	22	23	24	25	26	27	28	29	30					
14	15	16	17	18	19	20	21	22	23	24	25	26	27	28	29	30	31		

*yearly*OVERVIEW

JANUARY			FEBRUARY			MARCH		
1	T		1	F		1	F	
2	W		2	S		2	S	
3	T		3	S		3	S	
4	F		4	M		4	M	
5	S		5	T		5	T	
6	S		6	W		6	W	
7	M		7	T		7	T	
8	T		8	F		8	F	
9	W		9	S		9	S	
10	T		10	S		10	S	
11	F		11	M		11	M	
12	S		12	T		12	T	
13	S		13	W		13	W	
14	M		14	T		14	T	
15	T		15	F		15	F	
16	W		16	S		16	S	
17	T		17	S		17	S	
18	F		18	M		18	M	
19	S		19	T		19	T	
20	S		20	W		20	W	
21	M		21	T		21	T	
22	T		22	F		22	F	
23	W		23	S		23	S	
24	T		24	S		24	S	
25	F		25	M		25	M	
26	S		26	T		26	T	
27	S		27	W		27	W	
28	M		28	T		28	T	
29	T					29	F	
30	W					30	S	
31	T					31	S	

2019

APRIL			MAY			JUNE		
1	M		1	W		1	S	
2	T		2	T		2	S	
3	W		3	F		3	M	
4	T		4	S		4	T	
5	F		5	S		5	W	
6	S		6	M		6	T	
7	S		7	T		7	F	
8	M		8	W		8	S	
9	T		9	T		9	S	
10	W		10	F		10	M	
11	T		11	S		11	T	
12	F		12	S		12	W	
13	S		13	M		13	T	
14	S		14	T		14	F	
15	M		15	W		15	S	
16	T		16	T		16	S	
17	W		17	F		17	M	
18	T		18	S		18	T	
19	F		19	S		19	W	
20	S		20	M		20	T	
21	S		21	T		21	F	
22	M		22	W		22	S	
23	T		23	T		23	S	
24	W		24	F		24	M	
25	T		25	S		25	T	
26	F		26	S		26	W	
27	S		27	M		27	T	
28	S		28	T		28	F	
29	M		29	W		29	S	
30	T		30	T		30	S	
			31	F				

*yearly*OVERVIEW

JULY			AUGUST			SEPTEMBER		
1	M		1	T		1	S	
2	T		2	F		2	M	
3	W		3	S		3	T	
4	T		4	S		4	W	
5	F		5	M		5	T	
6	S		6	T		6	F	
7	S		7	W		7	S	
8	M		8	T		8	S	
9	T		9	F		9	M	
10	W		10	S		10	T	
11	T		11	S		11	W	
12	F		12	M		12	T	
13	S		13	T		13	F	
14	S		14	W		14	S	
15	M		15	T		15	S	
16	T		16	F		16	M	
17	W		17	S		17	T	
18	T		18	S		18	W	
19	F		19	M		19	T	
20	S		20	T		20	F	
21	S		21	W		21	S	
22	M		22	T		22	S	
23	T		23	F		23	M	
24	W		24	S		24	T	
25	T		25	S		25	W	
26	F		26	M		26	T	
27	S		27	T		27	F	
28	S		28	W		28	S	
29	M		29	T		29	S	
30	T		30	F		30	M	
31	W		31	S				

16

2019

OCTOBER NOVEMBER DECEMBER

OCT			NOV			DEC		
1	T		1	F		1	S	
2	W		2	S		2	M	
3	T		3	S		3	T	
4	F		4	M		4	W	
5	S		5	T		5	T	
6	S		6	W		6	F	
7	M		7	T		7	S	
8	T		8	F		8	S	
9	W		9	S		9	M	
10	T		10	S		10	T	
11	F		11	M		11	W	
12	S		12	T		12	T	
13	S		13	W		13	F	
14	M		14	T		14	S	
15	T		15	F		15	S	
16	W		16	S		16	M	
17	T		17	S		17	T	
18	F		18	M		18	W	
19	S		19	T		19	T	
20	S		20	W		20	F	
21	M		21	T		21	S	
22	T		22	F		22	S	
23	W		23	S		23	M	
24	T		24	S		24	T	
25	F		25	M		25	W	
26	S		26	T		26	T	
27	S		27	W		27	F	
28	M		28	T		28	S	
29	T		29	F		29	S	
30	W		30	S		30	M	
31	T					31	T	

17

*monthly*PLAN

THIS WEEK	MON	TUE	WED
☐		1	2
☐			
☐			
☐	7	8	9
☐			
☐			
☐	14	15	16
☐			
☐			
☐	21	22	23
☐			
☐			
☐	28	29	30
☐			
☐			
☐			
☐			
☐			

THUR	FRI	SAT	SUN
3	4	5	6
10	11	12	13
17	18	19	20
24	25	26	27
31			

*monthly*TASKS

- [ ]
- [ ]
- [ ]
- [ ]
- [ ]
- [ ]
- [ ]
- [ ]
- [ ]
- [ ]
- [ ]
- [ ]
- [ ]
- [ ]
- [ ]
- [ ]
- [ ]
- [ ]
- [ ]
- [ ]
- [ ]
- [ ]
- [ ]
- [ ]
- [ ]
- [ ]
- [ ]
- [ ]
- [ ]

*monthly*TRACKER

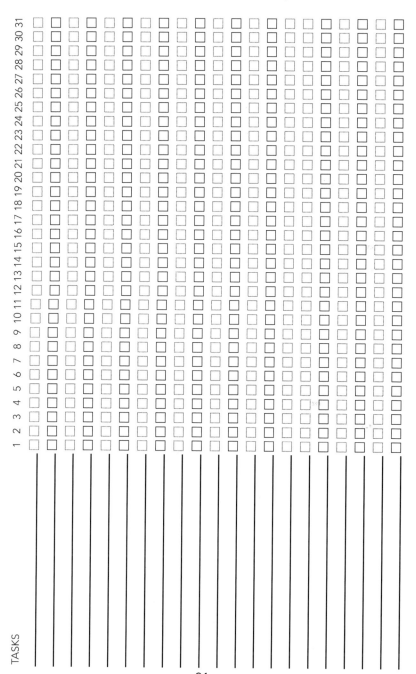

1 2 3 4 5 6 7 8 9 10 11 12 13 14 15 16 17 18 19 20 21 22 23 24 25 26 27 28 29 30 31

TASKS

*weekly*PLAN

31	1	2
MONDAY	TUESDAY	WEDNESDAY

☐ _____ ☐ _____ ☐ _____

☐ _____ ☐ _____ ☐ _____

☐ _____ ☐ _____ ☐ _____

December 31st, 2018 - January 6th, 2019

3	4	5
THURSDAY	FRIDAY	SATURDAY

☐ _____   ☐ _____   ☐ _____

☐ _____   ☐ _____   ☐ _____

☐ _____   ☐ _____   ☐ _____

6
SUNDAY

☐ _____

☐ _____

☐ _____

*weekly*PLAN

7	8	9
MONDAY	TUESDAY	WEDNESDAY

☐ _____
☐ _____
☐ _____

☐ _____
☐ _____
☐ _____

☐ _____
☐ _____
☐ _____

10	11	12
THURSDAY	FRIDAY	SATURDAY

☐ _____   ☐ _____   ☐ _____

☐ _____   ☐ _____   ☐ _____

☐ _____   ☐ _____   ☐ _____

13

SUNDAY

☐ _____

☐ _____

☐ _____

_weekly_PLAN

14	15	16
MONDAY	TUESDAY	WEDNESDAY

MONDAY
☐ _____
☐ _____
☐ _____

_____
_____
_____
_____
_____
_____
_____
_____
_____
_____
_____
_____
_____
_____

TUESDAY
☐ _____
☐ _____
☐ _____

_____
_____
_____
_____
_____
_____
_____
_____
_____
_____
_____
_____
_____
_____

WEDNESDAY
☐ _____
☐ _____
☐ _____

_____
_____
_____
_____
_____
_____
_____
_____
_____
_____
_____
_____
_____
_____

17	18	19
THURSDAY	FRIDAY	SATURDAY

☐ _____

☐ _____

☐ _____

_____

_____

_____

_____

_____

_____

_____

_____

_____

_____

_____

_____

_____

_____

20

SUNDAY

☐ _____

☐ _____

☐ _____

*weekly*PLAN

21	22	23
MONDAY	TUESDAY	WEDNESDAY

☐ _____
☐ _____
☐ _____

☐ _____
☐ _____
☐ _____

☐ _____
☐ _____
☐ _____

24	25	26
THURSDAY	FRIDAY	SATURDAY

☐ _____   ☐ _____   ☐ _____

☐ _____   ☐ _____   ☐ _____

☐ _____   ☐ _____   ☐ _____

27

SUNDAY

☐ _____

☐ _____

☐ _____

*weekly*PLAN

28	29	30
MONDAY	TUESDAY	WEDNESDAY

☐ _____
☐ _____
☐ _____

☐ _____
☐ _____
☐ _____

☐ _____
☐ _____
☐ _____

January 28th- February 3rd, 2019

31	1	2
THURSDAY	FRIDAY	SATURDAY

THURSDAY
- ☐ _____
- ☐ _____
- ☐ _____

_____
_____
_____
_____
_____
_____
_____
_____
_____
_____
_____
_____
_____
_____
_____

FRIDAY
- ☐ _____
- ☐ _____
- ☐ _____

_____
_____
_____
_____
_____
_____
_____
_____
_____
_____
_____

SATURDAY
- ☐ _____
- ☐ _____
- ☐ _____

3
SUNDAY
- ☐ _____
- ☐ _____
- ☐ _____

*monthly*PLAN

THIS WEEK	MON	TUE	WED
☐ _____	☐	☐	☐
☐ _____			
☐ _____			
☐ _____	4	5	6
☐ _____			
☐ _____			
☐ _____	11	12	13
☐ _____			
☐ _____			
☐ _____	18	19	20
☐ _____			
☐ _____			
☐ _____	25	26	27
☐ _____			
☐ _____			
☐ _____	☐	☐	☐
☐ _____			
☐ _____			

February 2019

THUR	FRI	SAT	SUN
	1	2	3
7	8	9	10
14	15	16	17
21	22	23	24
28			

*monthly*TASKS

- [ ]
- [ ]
- [ ]
- [ ]
- [ ]
- [ ]
- [ ]
- [ ]
- [ ]
- [ ]
- [ ]
- [ ]
- [ ]
- [ ]
- [ ]
- [ ]
- [ ]
- [ ]
- [ ]
- [ ]
- [ ]
- [ ]
- [ ]
- [ ]
- [ ]
- [ ]
- [ ]
- [ ]
- [ ]
- [ ]
- [ ]

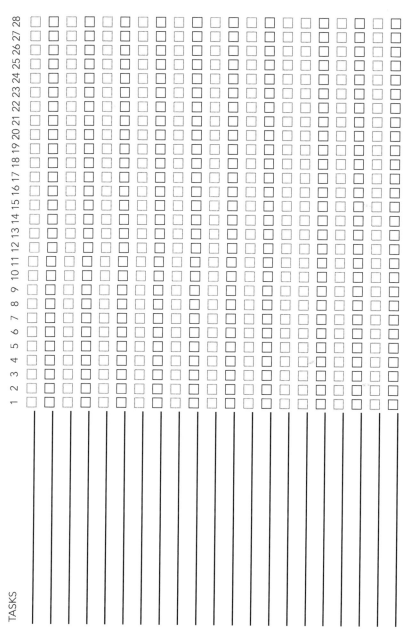

1 2 3 4 5 6 7 8 9 10 11 12 13 14 15 16 17 18 19 20 21 22 23 24 25 26 27 28

TASKS

*weekly*PLAN

4	5	6
MONDAY	TUESDAY	WEDNESDAY

☐ _____
☐ _____
☐ _____

☐ _____
☐ _____
☐ _____

☐ _____
☐ _____
☐ _____

7	8	9
THURSDAY	FRIDAY	SATURDAY

☐ _____

☐ _____

☐ _____

_____

_____

_____

_____

_____

_____

_____

_____

_____

_____

_____

		10
		SUNDAY

☐ _____

☐ _____

☐ _____

*weekly*PLAN

11	12	13
MONDAY	TUESDAY	WEDNESDAY

☐ _____   ☐ _____   ☐ _____

☐ _____   ☐ _____   ☐ _____

☐ _____   ☐ _____   ☐ _____

14	15	16
THURSDAY	FRIDAY	SATURDAY

☐ _____
☐ _____
☐ _____

☐ _____
☐ _____
☐ _____

☐ _____
☐ _____
☐ _____

17

SUNDAY

☐ _____
☐ _____
☐ _____

*weekly*PLAN

18	19	20
MONDAY	TUESDAY	WEDNESDAY

☐ _____

☐ _____

☐ _____

☐ _____

☐ _____

☐ _____

☐ _____

☐ _____

☐ _____

21	22	23
THURSDAY	FRIDAY	SATURDAY

☐ _____   ☐ _____   ☐ _____

☐ _____   ☐ _____   ☐ _____

☐ _____   ☐ _____   ☐ _____

	24
	SUNDAY

☐ _____

☐ _____

☐ _____

*weekly*PLAN

25	26	27
MONDAY	TUESDAY	WEDNESDAY

☐ _____
☐ _____
☐ _____

☐ _____
☐ _____
☐ _____

☐ _____
☐ _____
☐ _____

February 25th- March 3rd, 2019

28	1	2
THURSDAY	FRIDAY	SATURDAY

28 THURSDAY

☐ _____
☐ _____
☐ _____

_____
_____
_____
_____
_____
_____
_____
_____
_____
_____
_____
_____
_____
_____
_____
_____

1 FRIDAY

☐ _____
☐ _____
☐ _____

_____
_____
_____
_____
_____
_____
_____
_____
_____
_____
_____
_____
_____
_____
_____
_____

2 SATURDAY

☐ _____
☐ _____
☐ _____

3 SUNDAY

☐ _____
☐ _____
☐ _____

*monthly*PLAN

THIS WEEK	MON	TUE	WED
☐ _____	☐	☐	☐
☐ _____			
☐ _____			
☐ _____	4	5	6
☐ _____			
☐ _____			
☐ _____	11	12	13
☐ _____			
☐ _____			
☐ _____	18	19	20
☐ _____			
☐ _____			
☐ _____	25	26	27
☐ _____			
☐ _____			
☐ _____	☐	☐	☐
☐ _____			
☐ _____			

March 2019

THUR	FRI	SAT	SUN
	1	2	3
7	8	9	10
14	15	16	17
21	22	23	24
28	29	30	31

*monthly*TASKS

- [ ]
- [ ]
- [ ]
- [ ]
- [ ]
- [ ]
- [ ]
- [ ]
- [ ]
- [ ]
- [ ]
- [ ]
- [ ]
- [ ]
- [ ]
- [ ]
- [ ]
- [ ]
- [ ]
- [ ]
- [ ]
- [ ]
- [ ]
- [ ]
- [ ]
- [ ]
- [ ]
- [ ]
- [ ]
- [ ]

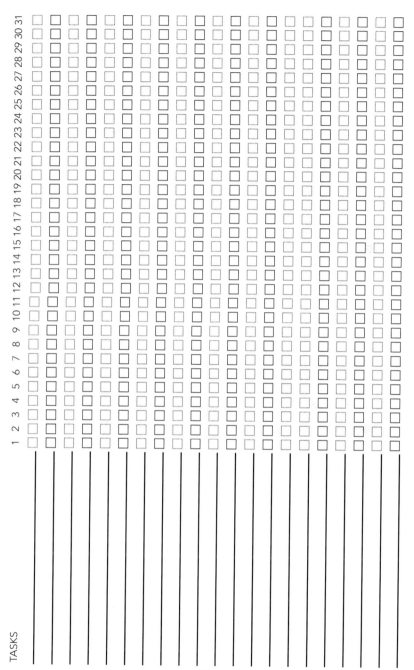

1 2 3 4 5 6 7 8 9 10 11 12 13 14 15 16 17 18 19 20 21 22 23 24 25 26 27 28 29 30 31

TASKS

*weekly*PLAN

4	5	6
MONDAY	TUESDAY	WEDNESDAY

☐ _____
☐ _____
☐ _____

☐ _____
☐ _____
☐ _____

☐ _____
☐ _____
☐ _____

March 4th- 10th, 2019

7	8	9
THURSDAY	FRIDAY	SATURDAY

☐ _____
☐ _____
☐ _____

☐ _____
☐ _____
☐ _____

☐ _____
☐ _____
☐ _____

10

SUNDAY

☐ _____
☐ _____
☐ _____

*weekly*PLAN

11	12	13
MONDAY	TUESDAY	WEDNESDAY

☐ _____ ☐ _____ ☐ _____

☐ _____ ☐ _____ ☐ _____

☐ _____ ☐ _____ ☐ _____

March 11th- 17th, 2019

14
THURSDAY

☐_____
☐_____
☐_____

_____
_____
_____
_____
_____
_____
_____
_____
_____
_____
_____
_____

15
FRIDAY

☐_____
☐_____
☐_____

_____
_____
_____
_____
_____
_____
_____
_____
_____
_____
_____
_____

16
SATURDAY

☐_____
☐_____
☐_____

17
SUNDAY

☐_____
☐_____
☐_____

*weekly*PLAN

18	19	20
MONDAY	TUESDAY	WEDNESDAY

18 — MONDAY

- ☐ _____
- ☐ _____
- ☐ _____

_____
_____
_____
_____
_____
_____
_____
_____
_____
_____
_____
_____
_____
_____
_____

19 — TUESDAY

- ☐ _____
- ☐ _____
- ☐ _____

_____
_____
_____
_____
_____
_____
_____
_____
_____
_____
_____
_____
_____
_____

20 — WEDNESDAY

- ☐ _____
- ☐ _____
- ☐ _____

_____
_____
_____
_____
_____
_____
_____
_____
_____
_____
_____
_____
_____

March 18th- 24th, 2019

21
THURSDAY

- [ ]
- [ ]
- [ ]

22
FRIDAY

- [ ]
- [ ]
- [ ]

23
SATURDAY

- [ ]
- [ ]
- [ ]

24
SUNDAY

- [ ]
- [ ]
- [ ]

*weekly*PLAN

25	26	27
MONDAY	TUESDAY	WEDNESDAY

MONDAY
- ☐ _____
- ☐ _____
- ☐ _____

_____
_____
_____
_____
_____
_____
_____
_____
_____
_____
_____
_____
_____

TUESDAY
- ☐ _____
- ☐ _____
- ☐ _____

_____
_____
_____
_____
_____
_____
_____
_____
_____
_____
_____
_____

WEDNESDAY
- ☐ _____
- ☐ _____
- ☐ _____

_____
_____
_____
_____
_____
_____
_____
_____
_____
_____
_____

28
THURSDAY

☐ _____
☐ _____
☐ _____

_____
_____
_____
_____
_____
_____
_____
_____
_____
_____
_____
_____
_____

29
FRIDAY

☐ _____
☐ _____
☐ _____

_____
_____
_____
_____
_____
_____
_____
_____
_____
_____
_____
_____
_____

30
SATURDAY

☐ _____
☐ _____
☐ _____

31
SUNDAY

☐ _____
☐ _____
☐ _____

*monthly*PLAN

THIS WEEK	MON	TUE	WED
☐	1	2	3
☐			
☐			
☐	8	9	10
☐			
☐			
☐	15	16	17
☐			
☐			
☐	22	23	24
☐			
☐			
☐	29	30	☐
☐			
☐			
☐	☐	☐	☐
☐			
☐			

THUR	FRI	SAT	SUN
4	5	6	7
11	12	13	14
18	19	20	21
25	26	27	28

*monthly*TASKS

- [ ]
- [ ]
- [ ]
- [ ]
- [ ]
- [ ]
- [ ]
- [ ]
- [ ]
- [ ]
- [ ]
- [ ]
- [ ]
- [ ]
- [ ]
- [ ]
- [ ]
- [ ]
- [ ]
- [ ]
- [ ]
- [ ]
- [ ]
- [ ]
- [ ]
- [ ]

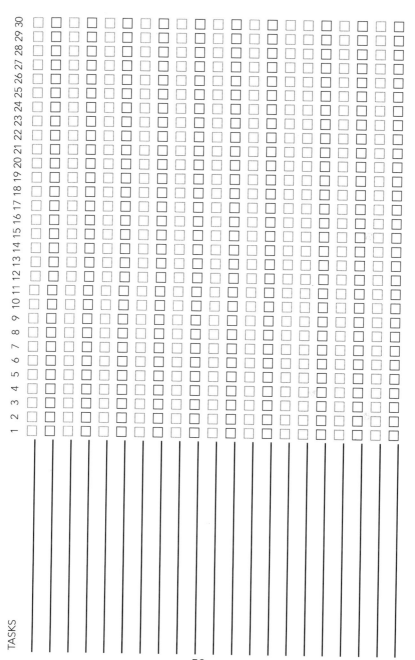

TASKS

*weekly*PLAN

1	2	3
MONDAY	TUESDAY	WEDNESDAY

☐ _____
☐ _____
☐ _____

☐ _____
☐ _____
☐ _____

☐ _____
☐ _____
☐ _____

4

THURSDAY

☐ _____
☐ _____
☐ _____

_____
_____
_____
_____
_____
_____
_____
_____
_____
_____
_____
_____
_____
_____
_____
_____
_____

5

FRIDAY

☐ _____
☐ _____
☐ _____

_____
_____
_____
_____
_____
_____
_____
_____
_____
_____
_____
_____
_____
_____
_____

6

SATURDAY

☐ _____
☐ _____
☐ _____

7

SUNDAY

☐ _____
☐ _____
☐ _____

*weekly*PLAN

8	9	10
MONDAY	TUESDAY	WEDNESDAY

MONDAY

☐ _____
☐ _____
☐ _____

_____
_____
_____
_____
_____
_____
_____
_____
_____
_____
_____
_____
_____
_____
_____
_____

TUESDAY

☐ _____
☐ _____
☐ _____

_____
_____
_____
_____
_____
_____
_____
_____
_____
_____
_____
_____
_____
_____
_____

WEDNESDAY

☐ _____
☐ _____
☐ _____

_____
_____
_____
_____
_____
_____
_____
_____
_____
_____
_____
_____
_____

11
THURSDAY

☐ _____
☐ _____
☐ _____

_____
_____
_____
_____
_____
_____
_____
_____
_____
_____
_____
_____
_____
_____

12
FRIDAY

☐ _____
☐ _____
☐ _____

_____
_____
_____
_____
_____
_____
_____
_____
_____
_____
_____
_____
_____

13
SATURDAY

☐ _____
☐ _____
☐ _____

14
SUNDAY

☐ _____
☐ _____
☐ _____

*weekly*PLAN

15	16	17
MONDAY	TUESDAY	WEDNESDAY

☐ _____ ☐ _____ ☐ _____

☐ _____ ☐ _____ ☐ _____

☐ _____ ☐ _____ ☐ _____

April 15th- 21st, 2019

18
THURSDAY

☐ _____
☐ _____
☐ _____

19
FRIDAY

☐ _____
☐ _____
☐ _____

20
SATURDAY

☐ _____
☐ _____
☐ _____

21
SUNDAY

☐ _____
☐ _____
☐ _____

*weekly*PLAN

22	23	24
MONDAY	TUESDAY	WEDNESDAY

☐ _____　　☐ _____　　☐ _____

☐ _____　　☐ _____　　☐ _____

☐ _____　　☐ _____　　☐ _____

25	26	27
THURSDAY	FRIDAY	SATURDAY

☐ _____   ☐ _____   ☐ _____

☐ _____   ☐ _____   ☐ _____

☐ _____   ☐ _____   ☐ _____

		28
		SUNDAY

☐ _____

☐ _____

☐ _____

*monthly*PLAN

THIS WEEK	MON	TUE	WED
☐			1
☐			
☐			
☐	6	7	8
☐			
☐			
☐	13	14	15
☐			
☐			
☐	20	21	22
☐			
☐			
☐	27	28	29
☐			
☐			
☐			
☐			
☐			

THUR	FRI	SAT	SUN
2	3	4	5
9	10	11	12
16	17	18	19
23	24	25	26
30	31		

*monthly*TASKS

- [ ]
- [ ]
- [ ]
- [ ]
- [ ]
- [ ]
- [ ]
- [ ]
- [ ]
- [ ]
- [ ]
- [ ]
- [ ]
- [ ]
- [ ]
- [ ]
- [ ]
- [ ]
- [ ]
- [ ]
- [ ]
- [ ]
- [ ]
- [ ]
- [ ]
- [ ]
- [ ]
- [ ]
- [ ]
- [ ]

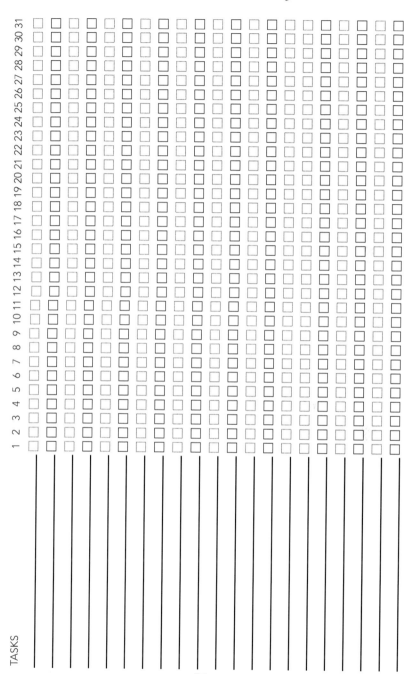

TASKS

1 2 3 4 5 6 7 8 9 10 11 12 13 14 15 16 17 18 19 20 21 22 23 24 25 26 27 28 29 30 31

*weekly*PLAN

29	30	1
MONDAY	TUESDAY	WEDNESDAY

☐ _____
☐ _____
☐ _____

☐ _____
☐ _____
☐ _____

☐ _____
☐ _____
☐ _____

2
THURSDAY

☐ _____
☐ _____
☐ _____

_____
_____
_____
_____
_____
_____
_____
_____
_____
_____
_____
_____
_____
_____
_____
_____
_____

3
FRIDAY

☐ _____
☐ _____
☐ _____

_____
_____
_____
_____
_____
_____
_____
_____
_____
_____
_____
_____
_____
_____
_____

4
SATURDAY

☐ _____
☐ _____
☐ _____

5
SUNDAY

☐ _____
☐ _____
☐ _____

*weekly*PLAN

6	7	8
MONDAY	TUESDAY	WEDNESDAY

☐ _____

☐ _____

☐ _____

_____

_____

_____

_____

_____

_____

_____

_____

_____

_____

_____

_____

_____

_____

9

THURSDAY

☐ _____
☐ _____
☐ _____

_____
_____
_____
_____
_____
_____
_____
_____
_____
_____
_____
_____
_____
_____
_____

10

FRIDAY

☐ _____
☐ _____
☐ _____

_____
_____
_____
_____
_____
_____
_____
_____
_____
_____
_____
_____
_____
_____

11

SATURDAY

☐ _____
☐ _____
☐ _____

12

SUNDAY

☐ _____
☐ _____
☐ _____

*weekly*PLAN

13	14	15
MONDAY	TUESDAY	WEDNESDAY

MONDAY
- ☐ _____
- ☐ _____
- ☐ _____

TUESDAY
- ☐ _____
- ☐ _____
- ☐ _____

WEDNESDAY
- ☐ _____
- ☐ _____
- ☐ _____

16	17	18
THURSDAY	FRIDAY	SATURDAY

16 — THURSDAY

☐ _____
☐ _____
☐ _____

_____
_____
_____
_____
_____
_____
_____
_____
_____
_____
_____
_____
_____
_____

17 — FRIDAY

☐ _____
☐ _____
☐ _____

_____
_____
_____
_____
_____
_____
_____
_____
_____
_____
_____
_____
_____
_____

18 — SATURDAY

☐ _____
☐ _____
☐ _____

19 — SUNDAY

☐ _____
☐ _____
☐ _____

*weekly*PLAN

20	21	22
MONDAY	TUESDAY	WEDNESDAY

MONDAY

☐ _____
☐ _____
☐ _____

TUESDAY

☐ _____
☐ _____
☐ _____

WEDNESDAY

☐ _____
☐ _____
☐ _____

23	24	25
THURSDAY	FRIDAY	SATURDAY

☐ _____   ☐ _____   ☐ _____

☐ _____   ☐ _____   ☐ _____

☐ _____   ☐ _____   ☐ _____

26

SUNDAY

☐ _____

☐ _____

☐ _____

*weekly*PLAN

27	28	29
MONDAY	TUESDAY	WEDNESDAY

☐ _____
☐ _____
☐ _____

☐ _____
☐ _____
☐ _____

☐ _____
☐ _____
☐ _____

30	31	1
THURSDAY	FRIDAY	SATURDAY

☐ _____

☐ _____

☐ _____

☐ _____

☐ _____

☐ _____

☐ _____

☐ _____

☐ _____

2

SUNDAY

☐ _____

☐ _____

☐ _____

*monthly*PLAN

THIS WEEK	MON	TUE	WED
☐	☐	☐	☐
☐			
☐			
☐	3	4	5
☐			
☐			
☐	10	11	12
☐			
☐			
☐	17	18	19
☐			
☐			
☐	24	25	26
☐			
☐			
☐	☐	☐	☐
☐			
☐			

June 2019

THUR	FRI	SAT	SUN
		1	2
6	7	8	9
13	14	15	16
20	21	22	23
27	28	29	30

*monthly*TASKS

☐ _____
☐ _____
☐ _____
☐ _____
☐ _____
☐ _____
☐ _____
☐ _____
☐ _____
☐ _____
☐ _____
☐ _____
☐ _____
☐ _____
☐ _____
☐ _____
☐ _____
☐ _____
☐ _____
☐ _____
☐ _____
☐ _____
☐ _____
☐ _____
☐ _____
☐ _____
☐ _____
☐ _____
☐ _____

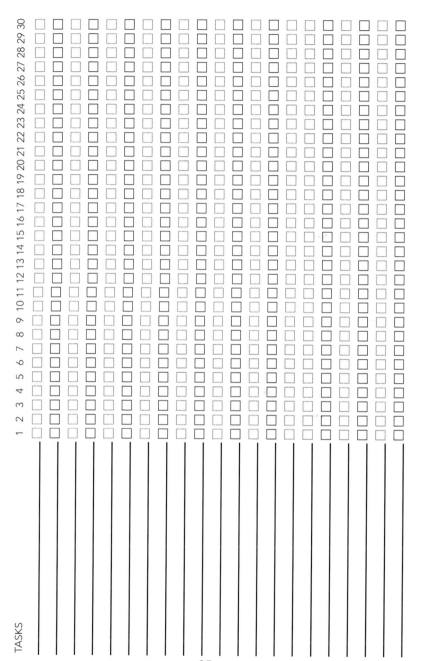

TASKS

1 2 3 4 5 6 7 8 9 10 11 12 13 14 15 16 17 18 19 20 21 22 23 24 25 26 27 28 29 30

*weekly*PLAN

3	4	5
MONDAY	TUESDAY	WEDNESDAY

☐ _____ ☐ _____ ☐ _____
☐ _____ ☐ _____ ☐ _____
☐ _____ ☐ _____ ☐ _____

6
THURSDAY

- ☐ _____
- ☐ _____
- ☐ _____

_____
_____
_____
_____
_____
_____
_____
_____
_____
_____
_____
_____
_____
_____
_____
_____

7
FRIDAY

- ☐ _____
- ☐ _____
- ☐ _____

_____
_____
_____
_____
_____
_____
_____
_____
_____
_____
_____
_____
_____
_____
_____
_____

8
SATURDAY

- ☐ _____
- ☐ _____
- ☐ _____

9
SUNDAY

- ☐ _____
- ☐ _____
- ☐ _____

*weekly*PLAN

10	11	12
MONDAY	TUESDAY	WEDNESDAY

MONDAY
- [ ] _____
- [ ] _____
- [ ] _____

TUESDAY
- [ ] _____
- [ ] _____
- [ ] _____

WEDNESDAY
- [ ] _____
- [ ] _____
- [ ] _____

13
THURSDAY

- [ ] _____
- [ ] _____
- [ ] _____

14
FRIDAY

- [ ] _____
- [ ] _____
- [ ] _____

15
SATURDAY

- [ ] _____
- [ ] _____
- [ ] _____

16
SUNDAY

- [ ] _____
- [ ] _____
- [ ] _____

*weekly*PLAN

17	18	19
MONDAY	TUESDAY	WEDNESDAY

☐ _____

☐ _____

☐ _____

☐ _____

☐ _____

☐ _____

☐ _____

☐ _____

☐ _____

June 17th- 23rd, 2019

20	21	22
THURSDAY	FRIDAY	SATURDAY

☐ _____
☐ _____
☐ _____

☐ _____
☐ _____
☐ _____

☐ _____
☐ _____
☐ _____

23
SUNDAY

☐ _____
☐ _____
☐ _____

91

*weekly*PLAN

24	25	26
MONDAY	TUESDAY	WEDNESDAY

☐ _____
☐ _____
☐ _____

☐ _____
☐ _____
☐ _____

☐ _____
☐ _____
☐ _____

27
THURSDAY

☐ _____
☐ _____
☐ _____

28
FRIDAY

☐ _____
☐ _____
☐ _____

29
SATURDAY

☐ _____
☐ _____
☐ _____

30
SUNDAY

☐ _____
☐ _____
☐ _____

*monthly*PLAN

THIS WEEK	MON	TUE	WED
☐	1	2	3
☐			
☐			
☐	8	9	10
☐			
☐			
☐	15	16	17
☐			
☐			
☐	22	23	24
☐			
☐			
☐	29	30	31
☐			
☐			
☐	☐	☐	☐
☐			
☐			

July 2019

THUR	FRI	SAT	SUN
4	5	6	7
11	12	13	14
18	19	20	21
25	26	27	28

*monthly*TASKS

☐ _____
☐ _____
☐ _____
☐ _____
☐ _____
☐ _____
☐ _____
☐ _____
☐ _____
☐ _____
☐ _____
☐ _____
☐ _____
☐ _____
☐ _____
☐ _____
☐ _____
☐ _____
☐ _____
☐ _____
☐ _____
☐ _____
☐ _____
☐ _____
☐ _____
☐ _____
☐ _____
☐ _____
☐ _____
☐ _____

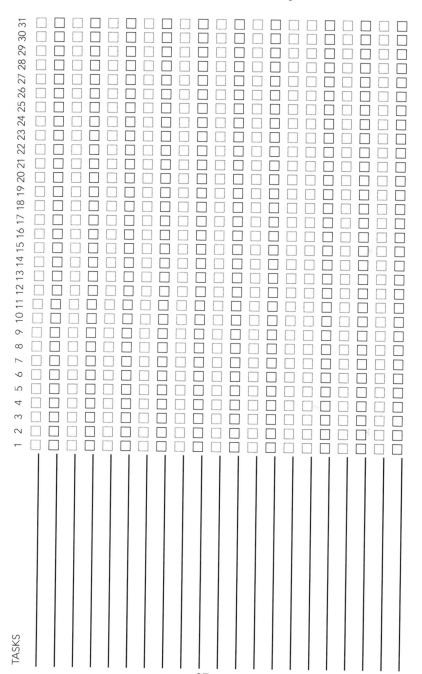

1 2 3 4 5 6 7 8 9 10 11 12 13 14 15 16 17 18 19 20 21 22 23 24 25 26 27 28 29 30 31

TASKS

*weekly*PLAN

1	2	3
MONDAY	TUESDAY	WEDNESDAY

☐ _____
☐ _____
☐ _____

☐ _____
☐ _____
☐ _____

☐ _____
☐ _____
☐ _____

July 1st- 7th, 2019

4	5	6
THURSDAY	FRIDAY	SATURDAY

☐ _____
☐ _____
☐ _____

☐ _____
☐ _____
☐ _____

☐ _____
☐ _____
☐ _____

7
SUNDAY

☐ _____
☐ _____
☐ _____

99

*weekly*PLAN

8	9	10
MONDAY	TUESDAY	WEDNESDAY

MONDAY
- ☐ _____
- ☐ _____
- ☐ _____

_____
_____
_____
_____
_____
_____
_____
_____
_____
_____
_____
_____
_____
_____
_____
_____

TUESDAY
- ☐ _____
- ☐ _____
- ☐ _____

_____
_____
_____
_____
_____
_____
_____
_____
_____
_____
_____
_____
_____
_____

WEDNESDAY
- ☐ _____
- ☐ _____
- ☐ _____

_____
_____
_____
_____
_____
_____
_____
_____
_____
_____
_____
_____
_____

July 8th- 14th, 2019

11
THURSDAY

☐ _____
☐ _____
☐ _____

_____
_____
_____
_____
_____
_____
_____
_____
_____
_____
_____
_____
_____
_____

12
FRIDAY

☐ _____
☐ _____
☐ _____

_____
_____
_____
_____
_____
_____
_____
_____
_____
_____
_____
_____

13
SATURDAY

☐ _____
☐ _____
☐ _____

14
SUNDAY

☐ _____
☐ _____
☐ _____

*weekly*PLAN

15	16	17
MONDAY	TUESDAY	WEDNESDAY

☐ _____
☐ _____
☐ _____

☐ _____
☐ _____
☐ _____

☐ _____
☐ _____
☐ _____

18
THURSDAY

☐ _____
☐ _____
☐ _____

_____
_____
_____
_____
_____
_____
_____
_____
_____
_____
_____
_____
_____
_____
_____

19
FRIDAY

☐ _____
☐ _____
☐ _____

_____
_____
_____
_____
_____
_____
_____
_____
_____
_____
_____
_____
_____
_____

20
SATURDAY

☐ _____
☐ _____
☐ _____

21
SUNDAY

☐ _____
☐ _____
☐ _____

*weekly*PLAN

22	23	24
MONDAY	TUESDAY	WEDNESDAY

☐ _____
☐ _____
☐ _____

☐ _____
☐ _____
☐ _____

☐ _____
☐ _____
☐ _____

25
THURSDAY

☐ _____
☐ _____
☐ _____

_____
_____
_____
_____
_____
_____
_____
_____
_____
_____
_____
_____
_____
_____

26
FRIDAY

☐ _____
☐ _____
☐ _____

_____
_____
_____
_____
_____
_____
_____
_____
_____
_____
_____
_____
_____
_____

27
SATURDAY

☐ _____
☐ _____
☐ _____

28
SUNDAY

☐ _____
☐ _____
☐ _____

*weekly*PLAN

29	30	31
MONDAY	TUESDAY	WEDNESDAY

☐ _____
☐ _____
☐ _____

☐ _____
☐ _____
☐ _____

☐ _____
☐ _____
☐ _____

1
THURSDAY

☐ _____
☐ _____
☐ _____

_____
_____
_____
_____
_____
_____
_____
_____
_____
_____
_____
_____
_____
_____
_____

2
FRIDAY

☐ _____
☐ _____
☐ _____

_____
_____
_____
_____
_____
_____
_____
_____
_____
_____
_____
_____
_____

3
SATURDAY

☐ _____
☐ _____
☐ _____

4
SUNDAY

☐ _____
☐ _____
☐ _____

*monthly*PLAN

THIS WEEK	MON	TUE	WED
☐	☐	☐	☐
☐			
☐			
☐	5	6	7
☐			
☐			
☐	12	13	14
☐			
☐			
☐	19	20	21
☐			
☐			
☐	26	27	28
☐			
☐			
☐	☐	☐	☐
☐			
☐			

THUR	FRI	SAT	SUN
1	2	3	4
8	9	10	11
15	16	17	18
22	23	24	25
29	30	31	

*monthly*TASKS

- [ ]
- [ ]
- [ ]
- [ ]
- [ ]
- [ ]
- [ ]
- [ ]
- [ ]
- [ ]
- [ ]
- [ ]
- [ ]
- [ ]
- [ ]
- [ ]
- [ ]
- [ ]
- [ ]
- [ ]
- [ ]
- [ ]
- [ ]
- [ ]
- [ ]
- [ ]
- [ ]
- [ ]
- [ ]
- [ ]

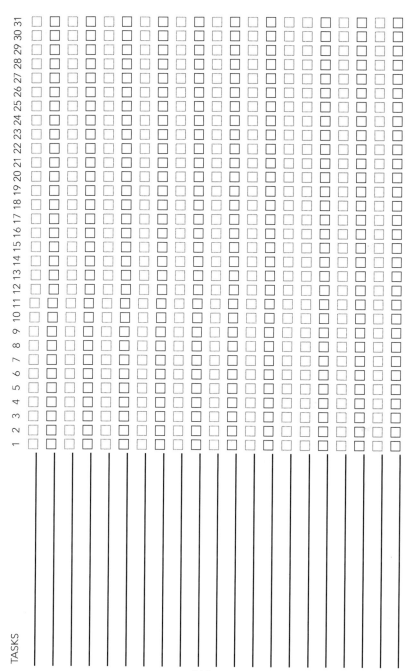

1 2 3 4 5 6 7 8 9 10 11 12 13 14 15 16 17 18 19 20 21 22 23 24 25 26 27 28 29 30 31

TASKS

111

*weekly*PLAN

5	6	7
MONDAY	TUESDAY	WEDNESDAY

☐ _____ ☐ _____ ☐ _____

☐ _____ ☐ _____ ☐ _____

☐ _____ ☐ _____ ☐ _____

8
THURSDAY

☐ _____
☐ _____
☐ _____

9
FRIDAY

☐ _____
☐ _____
☐ _____

10
SATURDAY

☐ _____
☐ _____
☐ _____

11
SUNDAY

☐ _____
☐ _____
☐ _____

*weekly*PLAN

12	13	14
MONDAY	TUESDAY	WEDNESDAY

☐ _____   ☐ _____   ☐ _____

☐ _____   ☐ _____   ☐ _____

☐ _____   ☐ _____   ☐ _____

15	16	17
THURSDAY	FRIDAY	SATURDAY

☐ _____
☐ _____
☐ _____

☐ _____
☐ _____
☐ _____

☐ _____
☐ _____
☐ _____

18
SUNDAY

☐ _____
☐ _____
☐ _____

*weekly*PLAN

19	20	21
MONDAY	TUESDAY	WEDNESDAY

MONDAY
- ☐ _____
- ☐ _____
- ☐ _____

_____
_____
_____
_____
_____
_____
_____
_____
_____
_____
_____
_____
_____
_____
_____
_____

TUESDAY
- ☐ _____
- ☐ _____
- ☐ _____

_____
_____
_____
_____
_____
_____
_____
_____
_____
_____
_____
_____
_____
_____
_____

WEDNESDAY
- ☐ _____
- ☐ _____
- ☐ _____

_____
_____
_____
_____
_____
_____
_____
_____
_____
_____
_____
_____
_____
_____

22	23	24
THURSDAY	FRIDAY	SATURDAY

☐ _____

☐ _____

☐ _____

☐ _____

☐ _____

☐ _____

☐ _____

☐ _____

☐ _____

25
SUNDAY

☐ _____

☐ _____

☐ _____

*weekly*PLAN

26	27	28
MONDAY	TUESDAY	WEDNESDAY

MONDAY

- ☐ _____
- ☐ _____
- ☐ _____

_____
_____
_____
_____
_____
_____
_____
_____
_____
_____
_____
_____
_____

TUESDAY

- ☐ _____
- ☐ _____
- ☐ _____

_____
_____
_____
_____
_____
_____
_____
_____
_____
_____
_____
_____
_____

WEDNESDAY

- ☐ _____
- ☐ _____
- ☐ _____

_____
_____
_____
_____
_____
_____
_____
_____
_____
_____
_____
_____
_____

August 26th- September 1st, 2019

29	30	31
THURSDAY	FRIDAY	SATURDAY

☐ _____   ☐ _____   ☐ _____
☐ _____   ☐ _____   ☐ _____
☐ _____   ☐ _____   ☐ _____

1
SUNDAY

☐ _____
☐ _____
☐ _____

119

*monthly*PLAN

THIS WEEK	MON	TUE	WED
☐			
☐			
☐			
☐	2	3	4
☐			
☐			
☐	9	10	11
☐			
☐			
☐	16	17	18
☐			
☐			
☐	23	24	25
☐			
☐			
☐	30		
☐			
☐			

September 2019

THUR	FRI	SAT	SUN
			1
5	6	7	8
12	13	14	15
19	20	21	22
26	27	28	29

*monthly*TASKS

- [ ]
- [ ]
- [ ]
- [ ]
- [ ]
- [ ]
- [ ]
- [ ]
- [ ]
- [ ]
- [ ]
- [ ]
- [ ]
- [ ]
- [ ]
- [ ]
- [ ]
- [ ]
- [ ]
- [ ]
- [ ]
- [ ]
- [ ]
- [ ]
- [ ]
- [ ]
- [ ]
- [ ]
- [ ]

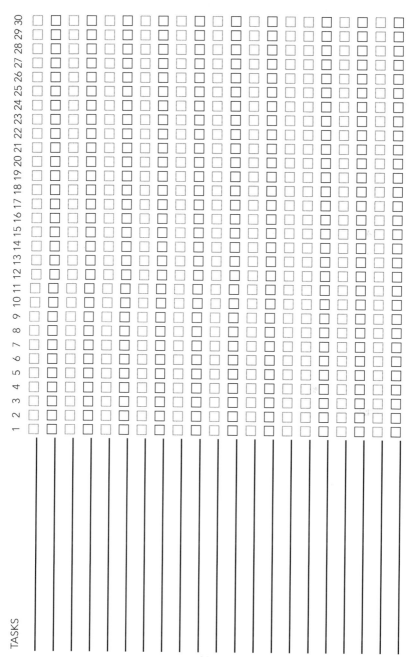

TASKS

*weekly*PLAN

2	3	4
MONDAY	TUESDAY	WEDNESDAY

☐ _____
☐ _____
☐ _____

☐ _____
☐ _____
☐ _____

☐ _____
☐ _____
☐ _____

September 2nd- 8th, 2019

5	6	7
THURSDAY	FRIDAY	SATURDAY

5
THURSDAY

☐ _____
☐ _____
☐ _____

6
FRIDAY

☐ _____
☐ _____
☐ _____

7
SATURDAY

☐ _____
☐ _____
☐ _____

8
SUNDAY

☐ _____
☐ _____
☐ _____

*weekly*PLAN

9	10	11
MONDAY	TUESDAY	WEDNESDAY

9 — MONDAY
- ☐ _____
- ☐ _____
- ☐ _____

10 — TUESDAY
- ☐ _____
- ☐ _____
- ☐ _____

11 — WEDNESDAY
- ☐ _____
- ☐ _____
- ☐ _____

12

THURSDAY

☐ _____
☐ _____
☐ _____

13

FRIDAY

☐ _____
☐ _____
☐ _____

14

SATURDAY

☐ _____
☐ _____
☐ _____

15

SUNDAY

☐ _____
☐ _____
☐ _____

*weekly*PLAN

16	17	18
MONDAY	TUESDAY	WEDNESDAY

☐ _____
☐ _____
☐ _____

☐ _____
☐ _____
☐ _____

☐ _____
☐ _____
☐ _____

September 16th- 22nd, 2019

19	20	21
THURSDAY	FRIDAY	SATURDAY

☐ _____ ☐ _____ ☐ _____

☐ _____ ☐ _____ ☐ _____

☐ _____ ☐ _____ ☐ _____

_____   _____

_____   _____

_____   _____

_____   _____

_____   _____

_____   _____

_____   _____

_____   _____   ## 22

                                     SUNDAY

_____   _____   ☐ _____

_____   _____   ☐ _____

_____   _____   ☐ _____

_____   _____

_____   _____

_____   _____

*weekly*PLAN

23	24	25
MONDAY	TUESDAY	WEDNESDAY

☐ _____
☐ _____
☐ _____

☐ _____
☐ _____
☐ _____

☐ _____
☐ _____
☐ _____

26
THURSDAY

☐ _____
☐ _____
☐ _____

27
FRIDAY

☐ _____
☐ _____
☐ _____

28
SATURDAY

☐ _____
☐ _____
☐ _____

29
SUNDAY

☐ _____
☐ _____
☐ _____

*monthly*PLAN

THIS WEEK	MON	TUE	WED
☐		1	2
☐			
☐			
☐	7	8	9
☐			
☐			
☐	14	15	16
☐			
☐			
☐	21	22	23
☐			
☐			
☐	28	29	30
☐			
☐			
☐			
☐			
☐			

THUR	FRI	SAT	SUN
3	4	5	6
10	11	12	13
17	18	19	20
24	25	26	27
31			

*monthly*TASKS

☐
☐
☐
☐
☐
☐
☐
☐
☐
☐
☐
☐
☐
☐
☐
☐
☐
☐
☐
☐
☐
☐
☐
☐
☐
☐
☐
☐
☐

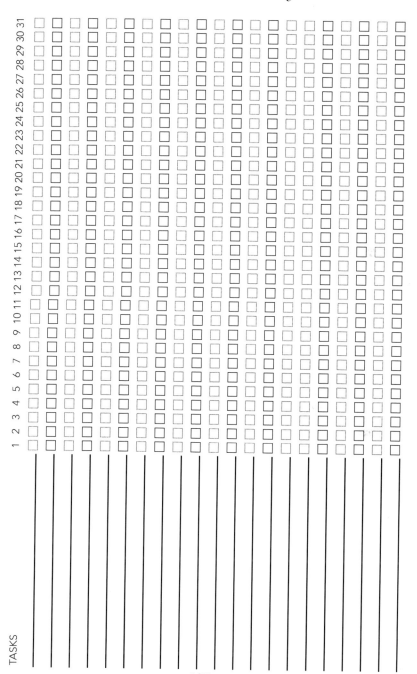

1 2 3 4 5 6 7 8 9 10 11 12 13 14 15 16 17 18 19 20 21 22 23 24 25 26 27 28 29 30 31

TASKS

weekly PLAN

30	1	2
MONDAY	TUESDAY	WEDNESDAY

☐ _____
☐ _____
☐ _____

☐ _____
☐ _____
☐ _____

☐ _____
☐ _____
☐ _____

3
THURSDAY

☐ _____
☐ _____
☐ _____

4
FRIDAY

☐ _____
☐ _____
☐ _____

5
SATURDAY

☐ _____
☐ _____
☐ _____

6
SUNDAY

☐ _____
☐ _____
☐ _____

*weekly*PLAN

7	8	9
MONDAY	TUESDAY	WEDNESDAY

MONDAY
- ☐ _____
- ☐ _____
- ☐ _____

TUESDAY
- ☐ _____
- ☐ _____
- ☐ _____

WEDNESDAY
- ☐ _____
- ☐ _____
- ☐ _____

October 7th- 13th, 2019

10
THURSDAY

☐ _____
☐ _____
☐ _____

11
FRIDAY

☐ _____
☐ _____
☐ _____

12
SATURDAY

☐ _____
☐ _____
☐ _____

13
SUNDAY

☐ _____
☐ _____
☐ _____

139

*weekly*PLAN

14	15	16
MONDAY	TUESDAY	WEDNESDAY

☐ _____

☐ _____

☐ _____

October 14th- 20th, 2019

17
THURSDAY

☐ _____
☐ _____
☐ _____

18
FRIDAY

☐ _____
☐ _____
☐ _____

19
SATURDAY

☐ _____
☐ _____
☐ _____

20
SUNDAY

☐ _____
☐ _____
☐ _____

*weekly*PLAN

21	22	23
MONDAY	TUESDAY	WEDNESDAY

MONDAY
- ☐ _____
- ☐ _____
- ☐ _____

TUESDAY
- ☐ _____
- ☐ _____
- ☐ _____

WEDNESDAY
- ☐ _____
- ☐ _____
- ☐ _____

October 21st- 27th, 2019

24
THURSDAY

☐_____
☐_____
☐_____

_____
_____
_____
_____
_____
_____
_____
_____
_____
_____
_____
_____
_____
_____

25
FRIDAY

☐_____
☐_____
☐_____

_____
_____
_____
_____
_____
_____
_____
_____
_____
_____
_____
_____
_____
_____

26
SATURDAY

☐_____
☐_____
☐_____

27
SUNDAY

☐_____
☐_____
☐_____

*weekly*PLAN

28	29	30
MONDAY	TUESDAY	WEDNESDAY

MONDAY
- ☐ _____
- ☐ _____
- ☐ _____

TUESDAY
- ☐ _____
- ☐ _____
- ☐ _____

WEDNESDAY
- ☐ _____
- ☐ _____
- ☐ _____

October 28th- November 3rd, 2019

31
THURSDAY

☐ _____
☐ _____
☐ _____

1
FRIDAY

☐ _____
☐ _____
☐ _____

2
SATURDAY

☐ _____
☐ _____
☐ _____

3
SUNDAY

☐ _____
☐ _____
☐ _____

*monthly*PLAN

THIS WEEK	MON	TUE	WED
☐	☐	☐	☐
☐			
☐			
☐	4	5	6
☐			
☐			
☐	11	12	13
☐			
☐			
☐	18	19	20
☐			
☐			
☐	25	26	27
☐			
☐			
☐	☐	☐	☐
☐			
☐			

November 2019

THUR	FRI	SAT	SUN
	1	2	3
7	8	9	10
14	15	16	17
21	22	23	24
28	29	30	

*monthly*TASKS

- ☐
- ☐
- ☐
- ☐
- ☐
- ☐
- ☐
- ☐
- ☐
- ☐
- ☐
- ☐
- ☐
- ☐
- ☐
- ☐
- ☐
- ☐
- ☐
- ☐
- ☐
- ☐
- ☐
- ☐
- ☐
- ☐
- ☐
- ☐

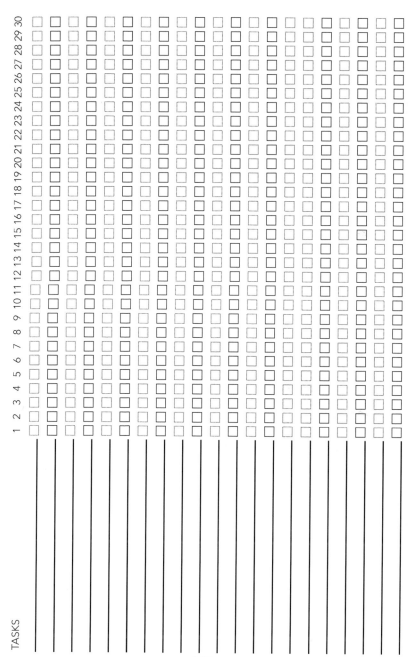

1 2 3 4 5 6 7 8 9 10 11 12 13 14 15 16 17 18 19 20 21 22 23 24 25 26 27 28 29 30

TASKS

*weekly*PLAN

4	5	6
MONDAY	TUESDAY	WEDNESDAY

MONDAY

☐ _____
☐ _____
☐ _____

TUESDAY

☐ _____
☐ _____
☐ _____

WEDNESDAY

☐ _____
☐ _____
☐ _____

7
THURSDAY

☐ _____
☐ _____
☐ _____

_____
_____
_____
_____
_____
_____
_____
_____
_____
_____
_____
_____

8
FRIDAY

☐ _____
☐ _____
☐ _____

_____
_____
_____
_____
_____
_____
_____
_____
_____
_____
_____

9
SATURDAY

☐ _____
☐ _____
☐ _____

10
SUNDAY

☐ _____
☐ _____
☐ _____

*weekly*PLAN

11	12	13
MONDAY	TUESDAY	WEDNESDAY

☐ _____
☐ _____
☐ _____

☐ _____
☐ _____
☐ _____

☐ _____
☐ _____
☐ _____

November 11th- 17th, 2019

14
THURSDAY

☐＿＿＿＿＿
☐＿＿＿＿＿
☐＿＿＿＿＿

15
FRIDAY

☐＿＿＿＿＿
☐＿＿＿＿＿
☐＿＿＿＿＿

16
SATURDAY

☐＿＿＿＿＿
☐＿＿＿＿＿
☐＿＿＿＿＿

17
SUNDAY

☐＿＿＿＿＿
☐＿＿＿＿＿
☐＿＿＿＿＿

*weekly*PLAN

18	19	20
MONDAY	TUESDAY	WEDNESDAY

☐ _____ ☐ _____ ☐ _____
☐ _____ ☐ _____ ☐ _____
☐ _____ ☐ _____ ☐ _____

21	22	23
THURSDAY	FRIDAY	SATURDAY

☐ _____
☐ _____
☐ _____

☐ _____
☐ _____
☐ _____

☐ _____
☐ _____
☐ _____

_____
_____
_____
_____
_____
_____
_____
_____
_____
_____
_____
_____
_____

_____
_____
_____
_____
_____
_____
_____
_____
_____
_____
_____
_____
_____

24
SUNDAY

☐ _____
☐ _____
☐ _____

*weekly*PLAN

25	26	27
MONDAY	TUESDAY	WEDNESDAY

☐ _____
☐ _____
☐ _____

☐ _____
☐ _____
☐ _____

☐ _____
☐ _____
☐ _____

November 25th- December 1st, 2019

28
THURSDAY

- ☐ _____
- ☐ _____
- ☐ _____

_____
_____
_____
_____
_____
_____
_____
_____
_____
_____
_____
_____

29
FRIDAY

- ☐ _____
- ☐ _____
- ☐ _____

_____
_____
_____
_____
_____
_____
_____
_____
_____
_____
_____

30
SATURDAY

- ☐ _____
- ☐ _____
- ☐ _____

1
SUNDAY

- ☐ _____
- ☐ _____
- ☐ _____

*monthly*PLAN

THIS WEEK	MON	TUE	WED
☐	☐	☐	☐
☐			
☐			
☐	2	3	4
☐			
☐			
☐	9	10	11
☐			
☐			
☐	16	17	18
☐			
☐			
☐	23	24	25
☐			
☐			
☐	30	31	☐
☐			
☐			

December 2019

THUR	FRI	SAT	SUN
			1
5	6	7	8
12	13	14	15
19	20	21	22
26	27	28	29

*monthly*TASKS

☐ _____
☐ _____
☐ _____
☐ _____
☐ _____
☐ _____
☐ _____
☐ _____
☐ _____
☐ _____
☐ _____
☐ _____
☐ _____
☐ _____
☐ _____
☐ _____
☐ _____
☐ _____
☐ _____
☐ _____
☐ _____
☐ _____
☐ _____
☐ _____
☐ _____
☐ _____
☐ _____
☐ _____
☐ _____

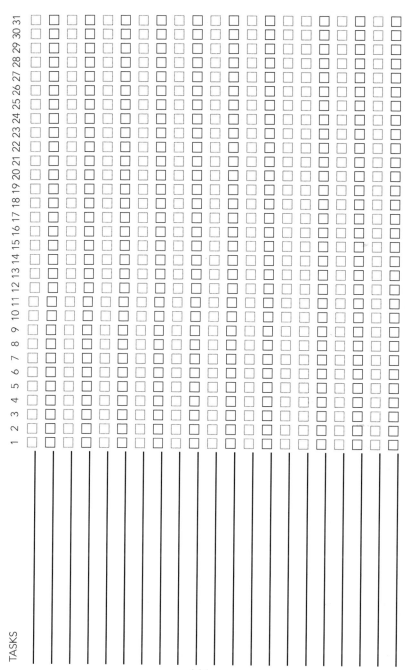

1 2 3 4 5 6 7 8 9 10 11 12 13 14 15 16 17 18 19 20 21 22 23 24 25 26 27 28 29 30 31

TASKS

*weekly*PLAN

2	3	4
MONDAY	TUESDAY	WEDNESDAY

☐ _____   ☐ _____   ☐ _____

☐ _____   ☐ _____   ☐ _____

☐ _____   ☐ _____   ☐ _____

December 2nd- 8th, 2019

5	6	7
THURSDAY	FRIDAY	SATURDAY

5
THURSDAY

☐ _____
☐ _____
☐ _____

_____
_____
_____
_____
_____
_____
_____
_____
_____
_____
_____
_____
_____
_____

6
FRIDAY

☐ _____
☐ _____
☐ _____

_____
_____
_____
_____
_____
_____
_____
_____
_____
_____
_____
_____
_____

7
SATURDAY

☐ _____
☐ _____
☐ _____

8
SUNDAY

☐ _____
☐ _____
☐ _____

*weekly*PLAN

9	10	11
MONDAY	TUESDAY	WEDNESDAY

MONDAY
- ☐ _____
- ☐ _____
- ☐ _____

TUESDAY
- ☐ _____
- ☐ _____
- ☐ _____

WEDNESDAY
- ☐ _____
- ☐ _____
- ☐ _____

12
THURSDAY

☐ _____
☐ _____
☐ _____

_____
_____
_____
_____
_____
_____
_____
_____
_____
_____
_____
_____
_____
_____

13
FRIDAY

☐ _____
☐ _____
☐ _____

_____
_____
_____
_____
_____
_____
_____
_____
_____
_____
_____
_____
_____

14
SATURDAY

☐ _____
☐ _____
☐ _____

15
SUNDAY

☐ _____
☐ _____
☐ _____

*weekly*PLAN

16	17	18
MONDAY	TUESDAY	WEDNESDAY

☐ _____ ☐ _____ ☐ _____

☐ _____ ☐ _____ ☐ _____

☐ _____ ☐ _____ ☐ _____

December 16th- 22nd, 2019

19
THURSDAY

☐
☐
☐

20
FRIDAY

☐
☐
☐

21
SATURDAY

☐
☐
☐

22
SUNDAY

☐
☐
☐

167

*weekly*PLAN

23	24	25
MONDAY	TUESDAY	WEDNESDAY

☐ _____
☐ _____
☐ _____

☐ _____
☐ _____
☐ _____

☐ _____
☐ _____
☐ _____

26	27	28
THURSDAY	FRIDAY	SATURDAY

☐ _____
☐ _____
☐ _____

☐ _____
☐ _____
☐ _____

☐ _____
☐ _____
☐ _____

29
SUNDAY

☐ _____
☐ _____
☐ _____

*weekly*PLAN

30	31	1
MONDAY	TUESDAY	WEDNESDAY

☐ _____

☐ _____

☐ _____

☐ _____

☐ _____

☐ _____

☐ _____

☐ _____

☐ _____

December 30th, 2019- January 5th, 2020

2	3	4
THURSDAY	FRIDAY	SATURDAY

☐ _____
☐ _____
☐ _____

☐ _____
☐ _____
☐ _____

☐ _____
☐ _____
☐ _____

5
SUNDAY

☐ _____
☐ _____
☐ _____

IMPORTANT PROJECTS

JAN	FEB	MAR	APR	MAY	JUN

SHORT TERM <1 MONTH PROJECTS

MID TERM 1-3 MONTH PROJECTS

LONG TERM 6+ MONTH PROJECTS

JUL AUG SEP OCT NOV DEC

175

*project*PLAN

PROJECT
_____

DESCRIPTION
_____
_____
_____

DUE DATE
_____

RESOURCES   TASKS

_____   ☐ _____
_____   ☐ _____
_____   ☐ _____
_____   ☐ _____
_____   ☐ _____
_____   ☐ _____
_____   ☐ _____
_____   ☐ _____
_____   ☐ _____
_____   ☐ _____
_____   ☐ _____
_____   ☐ _____
_____   ☐ _____
_____   ☐ _____
_____   ☐ _____
_____   ☐ _____
_____   ☐ _____
_____   ☐ _____
_____   ☐ _____

*project*PLAN

PROJECT

DESCRIPTION

DUE DATE

RESOURCES   TASKS

- [ ]
- [ ]
- [ ]
- [ ]
- [ ]
- [ ]
- [ ]
- [ ]
- [ ]
- [ ]
- [ ]
- [ ]
- [ ]
- [ ]
- [ ]
- [ ]
- [ ]
- [ ]
- [ ]

Project Notes

*project*PLAN

PROJECT _____

DESCRIPTION _____

_____

_____

_____

DUE DATE _____

RESOURCES   TASKS

_____   ☐ _____

_____   ☐ _____

_____   ☐ _____

_____   ☐ _____

_____   ☐ _____

_____   ☐ _____

_____   ☐ _____

_____   ☐ _____

_____   ☐ _____

_____   ☐ _____

_____   ☐ _____

_____   ☐ _____

_____   ☐ _____

_____   ☐ _____

_____   ☐ _____

_____   ☐ _____

_____   ☐ _____

_____   ☐ _____

_____   ☐ _____

_____   ☐ _____

*project*PLAN

PROJECT
_____

DESCRIPTION
_____
_____
_____
_____

DUE DATE
_____

RESOURCES　　　　　　TASKS

_____　☐ _____
_____　☐ _____
_____　☐ _____
_____　☐ _____
_____　☐ _____
_____　☐ _____
_____　☐ _____
_____　☐ _____
_____　☐ _____
_____　☐ _____
_____　☐ _____
_____　☐ _____
_____　☐ _____
_____　☐ _____
_____　☐ _____
_____　☐ _____
_____　☐ _____
_____　☐ _____
_____　☐ _____
_____　☐ _____

Project Notes

*project*PLAN

PROJECT

DESCRIPTION

DUE DATE

RESOURCES

TASKS

- [ ]
- [ ]
- [ ]
- [ ]
- [ ]
- [ ]
- [ ]
- [ ]
- [ ]
- [ ]
- [ ]
- [ ]
- [ ]
- [ ]
- [ ]
- [ ]
- [ ]
- [ ]
- [ ]
- [ ]

Project Notes

*project*PLAN

PROJECT

DESCRIPTION

DUE DATE

RESOURCES   TASKS

- [ ]
- [ ]
- [ ]
- [ ]
- [ ]
- [ ]
- [ ]
- [ ]
- [ ]
- [ ]
- [ ]
- [ ]
- [ ]
- [ ]
- [ ]
- [ ]
- [ ]
- [ ]
- [ ]
- [ ]

Project Notes

*project*PLAN

PROJECT

DESCRIPTION

DUE DATE

RESOURCES   TASKS

- ☐
- ☐
- ☐
- ☐
- ☐
- ☐
- ☐
- ☐
- ☐
- ☐
- ☐
- ☐
- ☐
- ☐
- ☐
- ☐
- ☐
- ☐
- ☐

Project Notes

*project*PLAN

PROJECT

DESCRIPTION

DUE DATE

RESOURCES   TASKS

- [ ]
- [ ]
- [ ]
- [ ]
- [ ]
- [ ]
- [ ]
- [ ]
- [ ]
- [ ]
- [ ]
- [ ]
- [ ]
- [ ]
- [ ]
- [ ]
- [ ]
- [ ]
- [ ]
- [ ]

Project Notes

*project*PLAN

PROJECT _____

DESCRIPTION _____

_____

_____

DUE DATE _____

RESOURCES   TASKS

_____   ☐ _____
_____   ☐ _____
_____   ☐ _____
_____   ☐ _____
_____   ☐ _____
_____   ☐ _____
_____   ☐ _____
_____   ☐ _____
_____   ☐ _____
_____   ☐ _____
_____   ☐ _____
_____   ☐ _____
_____   ☐ _____
_____   ☐ _____
_____   ☐ _____
_____   ☐ _____
_____   ☐ _____
_____   ☐ _____
_____   ☐ _____
_____   ☐ _____

Project Notes

*project*PLAN

PROJECT

DESCRIPTION

DUE DATE

RESOURCES   TASKS

- [ ]
- [ ]
- [ ]
- [ ]
- [ ]
- [ ]
- [ ]
- [ ]
- [ ]
- [ ]
- [ ]
- [ ]
- [ ]
- [ ]
- [ ]
- [ ]
- [ ]
- [ ]
- [ ]

*project*PLAN

PROJECT

DESCRIPTION

DUE DATE

RESOURCES   TASKS

- [ ]
- [ ]
- [ ]
- [ ]
- [ ]
- [ ]
- [ ]
- [ ]
- [ ]
- [ ]
- [ ]
- [ ]
- [ ]
- [ ]
- [ ]
- [ ]
- [ ]
- [ ]
- [ ]

Project Notes

*project*PLAN

PROJECT

DESCRIPTION

DUE DATE

RESOURCES   TASKS

- [ ]
- [ ]
- [ ]
- [ ]
- [ ]
- [ ]
- [ ]
- [ ]
- [ ]
- [ ]
- [ ]
- [ ]
- [ ]
- [ ]
- [ ]
- [ ]
- [ ]
- [ ]
- [ ]

Project Notes

*project*PLAN

PROJECT _____

DESCRIPTION _____

_____

_____

DUE DATE _____

RESOURCES   TASKS

_____   ☐ _____
_____   ☐ _____
_____   ☐ _____
_____   ☐ _____
_____   ☐ _____
_____   ☐ _____
_____   ☐ _____
_____   ☐ _____
_____   ☐ _____
_____   ☐ _____
_____   ☐ _____
_____   ☐ _____
_____   ☐ _____
_____   ☐ _____
_____   ☐ _____
_____   ☐ _____
_____   ☐ _____
_____   ☐ _____
_____   ☐ _____
_____   ☐ _____

*project*PLAN

PROJECT

DESCRIPTION

DUE DATE

RESOURCES   TASKS

- [ ]
- [ ]
- [ ]
- [ ]
- [ ]
- [ ]
- [ ]
- [ ]
- [ ]
- [ ]
- [ ]
- [ ]
- [ ]
- [ ]
- [ ]
- [ ]
- [ ]
- [ ]
- [ ]
- [ ]

*project*PLAN

PROJECT

DESCRIPTION

DUE DATE

RESOURCES   TASKS

- [ ]
- [ ]
- [ ]
- [ ]
- [ ]
- [ ]
- [ ]
- [ ]
- [ ]
- [ ]
- [ ]
- [ ]
- [ ]
- [ ]
- [ ]
- [ ]
- [ ]
- [ ]
- [ ]

*project*PLAN

PROJECT

DESCRIPTION

DUE DATE

RESOURCES   TASKS

- [ ]
- [ ]
- [ ]
- [ ]
- [ ]
- [ ]
- [ ]
- [ ]
- [ ]
- [ ]
- [ ]
- [ ]
- [ ]
- [ ]
- [ ]
- [ ]
- [ ]
- [ ]
- [ ]
- [ ]

Project Notes

*project*PLAN

PROJECT

DESCRIPTION

DUE DATE

RESOURCES   TASKS

☐
☐
☐
☐
☐
☐
☐
☐
☐
☐
☐
☐
☐
☐
☐
☐
☐
☐
☐
☐

Project Notes

*project*PLAN

PROJECT _____

DESCRIPTION _____

_____

_____

DUE DATE _____

RESOURCES   TASKS

RESOURCES	TASKS
_____	☐ _____
_____	☐ _____
_____	☐ _____
_____	☐ _____
_____	☐ _____
_____	☐ _____
_____	☐ _____
_____	☐ _____
_____	☐ _____
_____	☐ _____
_____	☐ _____
_____	☐ _____
_____	☐ _____
_____	☐ _____
_____	☐ _____
_____	☐ _____
_____	☐ _____
_____	☐ _____
_____	☐ _____

*project*PLAN

PROJECT

DESCRIPTION

DUE DATE

RESOURCES   TASKS

- [ ]
- [ ]
- [ ]
- [ ]
- [ ]
- [ ]
- [ ]
- [ ]
- [ ]
- [ ]
- [ ]
- [ ]
- [ ]
- [ ]
- [ ]
- [ ]
- [ ]
- [ ]
- [ ]

*project*PLAN

PROJECT
_____

DESCRIPTION
_____

_____

_____

_____

DUE DATE
_____

RESOURCES   TASKS

_____   ☐ _____

_____   ☐ _____

_____   ☐ _____

_____   ☐ _____

_____   ☐ _____

_____   ☐ _____

_____   ☐ _____

_____   ☐ _____

_____   ☐ _____

_____   ☐ _____

_____   ☐ _____

_____   ☐ _____

_____   ☐ _____

_____   ☐ _____

_____   ☐ _____

_____   ☐ _____

_____   ☐ _____

_____   ☐ _____

_____   ☐ _____

Project Notes

*project*PLAN

PROJECT

DESCRIPTION

DUE DATE

RESOURCES TASKS

- [ ]
- [ ]
- [ ]
- [ ]
- [ ]
- [ ]
- [ ]
- [ ]
- [ ]
- [ ]
- [ ]
- [ ]
- [ ]
- [ ]
- [ ]
- [ ]
- [ ]
- [ ]
- [ ]

*project*PLAN

PROJECT

DESCRIPTION

DUE DATE

RESOURCES   TASKS

- [ ]
- [ ]
- [ ]
- [ ]
- [ ]
- [ ]
- [ ]
- [ ]
- [ ]
- [ ]
- [ ]
- [ ]
- [ ]
- [ ]
- [ ]
- [ ]
- [ ]
- [ ]
- [ ]
- [ ]

Project Notes

*project*PLAN

PROJECT _____

DESCRIPTION _____

_____

_____

_____

DUE DATE _____

RESOURCES   TASKS

RESOURCES	TASKS
_____	☐ _____
_____	☐ _____
_____	☐ _____
_____	☐ _____
_____	☐ _____
_____	☐ _____
_____	☐ _____
_____	☐ _____
_____	☐ _____
_____	☐ _____
_____	☐ _____
_____	☐ _____
_____	☐ _____
_____	☐ _____
_____	☐ _____
_____	☐ _____
_____	☐ _____
_____	☐ _____
_____	☐ _____
_____	☐ _____

Project Notes

*project*PLAN

PROJECT

DESCRIPTION

DUE DATE

RESOURCES

TASKS

- [ ]
- [ ]
- [ ]
- [ ]
- [ ]
- [ ]
- [ ]
- [ ]
- [ ]
- [ ]
- [ ]
- [ ]
- [ ]
- [ ]
- [ ]
- [ ]
- [ ]
- [ ]
- [ ]
- [ ]

Project Notes

*project*PLAN

PROJECT

DESCRIPTION

DUE DATE

RESOURCES   TASKS

☐
☐
☐
☐
☐
☐
☐
☐
☐
☐
☐
☐
☐
☐
☐
☐
☐
☐
☐
☐

Project Notes

*project*PLAN

PROJECT

DESCRIPTION

DUE DATE

RESOURCES   TASKS

☐
☐
☐
☐
☐
☐
☐
☐
☐
☐
☐
☐
☐
☐
☐
☐
☐
☐
☐
☐

Project Notes

*project*PLAN

PROJECT

DESCRIPTION

DUE DATE

RESOURCES   TASKS

☐
☐
☐
☐
☐
☐
☐
☐
☐
☐
☐
☐
☐
☐
☐
☐
☐
☐
☐
☐

Project Notes

*project*PLAN

PROJECT

DESCRIPTION

DUE DATE

RESOURCES   TASKS

- [ ]
- [ ]
- [ ]
- [ ]
- [ ]
- [ ]
- [ ]
- [ ]
- [ ]
- [ ]
- [ ]
- [ ]
- [ ]
- [ ]
- [ ]
- [ ]
- [ ]
- [ ]
- [ ]
- [ ]

Project Notes

*project*PLAN

PROJECT

DESCRIPTION

DUE DATE

RESOURCES   TASKS

☐
☐
☐
☐
☐
☐
☐
☐
☐
☐
☐
☐
☐
☐
☐
☐
☐
☐
☐
☐

Project Notes

*project*PLAN

PROJECT

DESCRIPTION

DUE DATE

RESOURCES   TASKS

- [ ]
- [ ]
- [ ]
- [ ]
- [ ]
- [ ]
- [ ]
- [ ]
- [ ]
- [ ]
- [ ]
- [ ]
- [ ]
- [ ]
- [ ]
- [ ]
- [ ]
- [ ]
- [ ]
- [ ]

Project Notes

*project*PLAN

PROJECT

DESCRIPTION

DUE DATE

RESOURCES   TASKS

- [ ]
- [ ]
- [ ]
- [ ]
- [ ]
- [ ]
- [ ]
- [ ]
- [ ]
- [ ]
- [ ]
- [ ]
- [ ]
- [ ]
- [ ]
- [ ]
- [ ]
- [ ]
- [ ]
- [ ]

Project Notes

*project*PLAN

PROJECT

DESCRIPTION

DUE DATE

RESOURCES   TASKS

- ☐
- ☐
- ☐
- ☐
- ☐
- ☐
- ☐
- ☐
- ☐
- ☐
- ☐
- ☐
- ☐
- ☐
- ☐
- ☐
- ☐
- ☐
- ☐
- ☐

Project Notes

*project*PLAN

PROJECT
_____

DESCRIPTION
_____
_____
_____
_____

DUE DATE
_____

RESOURCES   TASKS

_____   ☐ _____
_____   ☐ _____
_____   ☐ _____
_____   ☐ _____
_____   ☐ _____
_____   ☐ _____
_____   ☐ _____
_____   ☐ _____
_____   ☐ _____
_____   ☐ _____
_____   ☐ _____
_____   ☐ _____
_____   ☐ _____
_____   ☐ _____
_____   ☐ _____
_____   ☐ _____
_____   ☐ _____
_____   ☐ _____
_____   ☐ _____
                          ☐

*project*PLAN

PROJECT

DESCRIPTION

DUE DATE

RESOURCES

TASKS

- [ ]
- [ ]
- [ ]
- [ ]
- [ ]
- [ ]
- [ ]
- [ ]
- [ ]
- [ ]
- [ ]
- [ ]
- [ ]
- [ ]
- [ ]
- [ ]
- [ ]
- [ ]
- [ ]
- [ ]

*project*PLAN

PROJECT _____

DESCRIPTION _____

_____

_____

DUE DATE _____

RESOURCES   TASKS

_____   ☐ _____
_____   ☐ _____
_____   ☐ _____
_____   ☐ _____
_____   ☐ _____
_____   ☐ _____
_____   ☐ _____
_____   ☐ _____
_____   ☐ _____
_____   ☐ _____
_____   ☐ _____
_____   ☐ _____
_____   ☐ _____
_____   ☐ _____
_____   ☐ _____
_____   ☐ _____
_____   ☐ _____
_____   ☐ _____
_____   ☐ _____
_____   ☐ _____

Project Notes

*project*PLAN

PROJECT

DESCRIPTION

DUE DATE

RESOURCES   TASKS

☐
☐
☐
☐
☐
☐
☐
☐
☐
☐
☐
☐
☐
☐
☐
☐
☐
☐
☐

*project*PLAN

PROJECT

DESCRIPTION

DUE DATE

RESOURCES   TASKS

- [ ]
- [ ]
- [ ]
- [ ]
- [ ]
- [ ]
- [ ]
- [ ]
- [ ]
- [ ]
- [ ]
- [ ]
- [ ]
- [ ]
- [ ]
- [ ]
- [ ]
- [ ]
- [ ]
- [ ]

*project*PLAN

PROJECT

DESCRIPTION

DUE DATE

RESOURCES   TASKS

☐
☐
☐
☐
☐
☐
☐
☐
☐
☐
☐
☐
☐
☐
☐
☐
☐
☐
☐
☐

Project Notes

*project*PLAN

PROJECT

DESCRIPTION

DUE DATE

RESOURCES   TASKS

☐
☐
☐
☐
☐
☐
☐
☐
☐
☐
☐
☐
☐
☐
☐
☐
☐
☐
☐
☐

Project Notes

*project*PLAN

PROJECT

DESCRIPTION

DUE DATE

RESOURCES   TASKS

- [ ]
- [ ]
- [ ]
- [ ]
- [ ]
- [ ]
- [ ]
- [ ]
- [ ]
- [ ]
- [ ]
- [ ]
- [ ]
- [ ]
- [ ]
- [ ]
- [ ]
- [ ]
- [ ]
- [ ]

Project Notes

BRILLIANT IDEAS

*brain*DUMP

- [ ]
- [ ]
- [ ]
- [ ]
- [ ]
- [ ]
- [ ]
- [ ]
- [ ]
- [ ]
- [ ]
- [ ]
- [ ]
- [ ]
- [ ]
- [ ]
- [ ]
- [ ]
- [ ]
- [ ]
- [ ]
- [ ]
- [ ]
- [ ]
- [ ]
- [ ]
- [ ]
- [ ]

Organize & Act   *date: __ / __ / ____*

IMPORTANT   NOT IMPORTANT

URGENT

NOT URGENT

*brain*DUMP

- [ ]
- [ ]
- [ ]
- [ ]
- [ ]
- [ ]
- [ ]
- [ ]
- [ ]
- [ ]
- [ ]
- [ ]
- [ ]
- [ ]
- [ ]
- [ ]
- [ ]
- [ ]
- [ ]
- [ ]
- [ ]
- [ ]
- [ ]
- [ ]
- [ ]
- [ ]
- [ ]
- [ ]
- [ ]

Organize & Act   *date: __ / __ / ____*

IMPORTANT

NOT IMPORTANT

URGENT

NOT URGENT

*brain*DUMP

- [ ]
- [ ]
- [ ]
- [ ]
- [ ]
- [ ]
- [ ]
- [ ]
- [ ]
- [ ]
- [ ]
- [ ]
- [ ]
- [ ]
- [ ]
- [ ]
- [ ]
- [ ]
- [ ]
- [ ]
- [ ]
- [ ]
- [ ]
- [ ]
- [ ]
- [ ]
- [ ]
- [ ]
- [ ]
- [ ]

Organize & Act   *date: __ / __ / ____*

IMPORTANT   NOT IMPORTANT

URGENT

NOT URGENT

*brain*DUMP

- [ ]
- [ ]
- [ ]
- [ ]
- [ ]
- [ ]
- [ ]
- [ ]
- [ ]
- [ ]
- [ ]
- [ ]
- [ ]
- [ ]
- [ ]
- [ ]
- [ ]
- [ ]
- [ ]
- [ ]
- [ ]
- [ ]
- [ ]
- [ ]
- [ ]
- [ ]
- [ ]
- [ ]

Organize & Act   *date: __ / __ / ____*

IMPORTANT   NOT IMPORTANT

URGENT

NOT URGENT

*brain*DUMP

☐
☐
☐
☐
☐
☐
☐
☐
☐
☐
☐
☐
☐
☐
☐
☐
☐
☐
☐
☐
☐
☐
☐
☐
☐
☐
☐
☐

Organize & Act   *date: __ / __ / ____*

IMPORTANT   NOT IMPORTANT

URGENT

NOT URGENT

*brain*DUMP

- [ ]
- [ ]
- [ ]
- [ ]
- [ ]
- [ ]
- [ ]
- [ ]
- [ ]
- [ ]
- [ ]
- [ ]
- [ ]
- [ ]
- [ ]
- [ ]
- [ ]
- [ ]
- [ ]
- [ ]
- [ ]
- [ ]
- [ ]
- [ ]
- [ ]
- [ ]
- [ ]
- [ ]

Organize & Act

date: __ / __ / ____

IMPORTANT

NOT IMPORTANT

URGENT

NOT URGENT

*brain*DUMP

- [ ]
- [ ]
- [ ]
- [ ]
- [ ]
- [ ]
- [ ]
- [ ]
- [ ]
- [ ]
- [ ]
- [ ]
- [ ]
- [ ]
- [ ]
- [ ]
- [ ]
- [ ]
- [ ]
- [ ]
- [ ]
- [ ]
- [ ]
- [ ]
- [ ]
- [ ]
- [ ]
- [ ]
- [ ]

Organize & Act   *date: __ / __ / ____*

IMPORTANT   NOT IMPORTANT

URGENT

NOT URGENT

*brain*DUMP

- [ ]
- [ ]
- [ ]
- [ ]
- [ ]
- [ ]
- [ ]
- [ ]
- [ ]
- [ ]
- [ ]
- [ ]
- [ ]
- [ ]
- [ ]
- [ ]
- [ ]
- [ ]
- [ ]
- [ ]
- [ ]
- [ ]
- [ ]
- [ ]
- [ ]
- [ ]
- [ ]
- [ ]

Organize & Act

IMPORTANT

NOT IMPORTANT

URGENT

NOT URGENT

*brain*DUMP

- [ ]
- [ ]
- [ ]
- [ ]
- [ ]
- [ ]
- [ ]
- [ ]
- [ ]
- [ ]
- [ ]
- [ ]
- [ ]
- [ ]
- [ ]
- [ ]
- [ ]
- [ ]
- [ ]
- [ ]
- [ ]
- [ ]
- [ ]
- [ ]
- [ ]
- [ ]
- [ ]
- [ ]

Organize & Act

IMPORTANT

NOT IMPORTANT

URGENT

NOT URGENT

*brain*DUMP

☐
☐
☐
☐
☐
☐
☐
☐
☐
☐
☐
☐
☐
☐
☐
☐
☐
☐
☐
☐
☐
☐
☐
☐
☐
☐
☐
☐
☐
☐

Organize & Act

IMPORTANT

NOT IMPORTANT

URGENT

NOT URGENT

*brain*DUMP

- [ ]
- [ ]
- [ ]
- [ ]
- [ ]
- [ ]
- [ ]
- [ ]
- [ ]
- [ ]
- [ ]
- [ ]
- [ ]
- [ ]
- [ ]
- [ ]
- [ ]
- [ ]
- [ ]
- [ ]
- [ ]
- [ ]
- [ ]
- [ ]
- [ ]
- [ ]
- [ ]

Organize & Act　　　*date:* __ / __ / ____

IMPORTANT　　　　　　　NOT IMPORTANT

URGENT

NOT URGENT

*brain*DUMP

- [ ]
- [ ]
- [ ]
- [ ]
- [ ]
- [ ]
- [ ]
- [ ]
- [ ]
- [ ]
- [ ]
- [ ]
- [ ]
- [ ]
- [ ]
- [ ]
- [ ]
- [ ]
- [ ]
- [ ]
- [ ]
- [ ]
- [ ]
- [ ]
- [ ]
- [ ]
- [ ]

Organize & Act   *date:* __ / __ / ____

IMPORTANT   NOT IMPORTANT

URGENT

NOT URGENT

*brain*DUMP

- [ ]
- [ ]
- [ ]
- [ ]
- [ ]
- [ ]
- [ ]
- [ ]
- [ ]
- [ ]
- [ ]
- [ ]
- [ ]
- [ ]
- [ ]
- [ ]
- [ ]
- [ ]
- [ ]
- [ ]
- [ ]
- [ ]
- [ ]
- [ ]
- [ ]
- [ ]
- [ ]
- [ ]

Organize & Act   *date: __ / __ / ____*

IMPORTANT   NOT IMPORTANT

URGENT

NOT URGENT

*brain*DUMP

- [ ]
- [ ]
- [ ]
- [ ]
- [ ]
- [ ]
- [ ]
- [ ]
- [ ]
- [ ]
- [ ]
- [ ]
- [ ]
- [ ]
- [ ]
- [ ]
- [ ]
- [ ]
- [ ]
- [ ]
- [ ]
- [ ]
- [ ]
- [ ]
- [ ]
- [ ]
- [ ]
- [ ]

Organize & Act

IMPORTANT

NOT IMPORTANT

URGENT

NOT URGENT

*brain*DUMP

- [ ]
- [ ]
- [ ]
- [ ]
- [ ]
- [ ]
- [ ]
- [ ]
- [ ]
- [ ]
- [ ]
- [ ]
- [ ]
- [ ]
- [ ]
- [ ]
- [ ]
- [ ]
- [ ]
- [ ]
- [ ]
- [ ]
- [ ]
- [ ]
- [ ]
- [ ]
- [ ]

Organize & Act   *date:* __ / __ / ____

IMPORTANT   NOT IMPORTANT

URGENT

NOT URGENT

*brain*DUMP

- [ ]
- [ ]
- [ ]
- [ ]
- [ ]
- [ ]
- [ ]
- [ ]
- [ ]
- [ ]
- [ ]
- [ ]
- [ ]
- [ ]
- [ ]
- [ ]
- [ ]
- [ ]
- [ ]
- [ ]
- [ ]
- [ ]
- [ ]
- [ ]
- [ ]
- [ ]
- [ ]
- [ ]

Organize & Act   *date:* __ / __ / ____

IMPORTANT   NOT IMPORTANT

URGENT

NOT URGENT

*brain*DUMP

- [ ]
- [ ]
- [ ]
- [ ]
- [ ]
- [ ]
- [ ]
- [ ]
- [ ]
- [ ]
- [ ]
- [ ]
- [ ]
- [ ]
- [ ]
- [ ]
- [ ]
- [ ]
- [ ]
- [ ]
- [ ]
- [ ]
- [ ]
- [ ]
- [ ]
- [ ]
- [ ]
- [ ]
- [ ]

Organize & Act

IMPORTANT

NOT IMPORTANT

URGENT

NOT URGENT

*brain*DUMP

- [ ]
- [ ]
- [ ]
- [ ]
- [ ]
- [ ]
- [ ]
- [ ]
- [ ]
- [ ]
- [ ]
- [ ]
- [ ]
- [ ]
- [ ]
- [ ]
- [ ]
- [ ]
- [ ]
- [ ]
- [ ]
- [ ]
- [ ]
- [ ]
- [ ]
- [ ]
- [ ]
- [ ]
- [ ]
- [ ]

Organize & Act   *date: __ / __ / ____*

IMPORTANT   NOT IMPORTANT

URGENT

NOT URGENT

*brain*DUMP

- [ ]
- [ ]
- [ ]
- [ ]
- [ ]
- [ ]
- [ ]
- [ ]
- [ ]
- [ ]
- [ ]
- [ ]
- [ ]
- [ ]
- [ ]
- [ ]
- [ ]
- [ ]
- [ ]
- [ ]
- [ ]
- [ ]
- [ ]
- [ ]
- [ ]
- [ ]
- [ ]

Organize & Act   *date:* __ / __ / ____

IMPORTANT

NOT IMPORTANT

URGENT

NOT URGENT

*brain*DUMP

- [ ]
- [ ]
- [ ]
- [ ]
- [ ]
- [ ]
- [ ]
- [ ]
- [ ]
- [ ]
- [ ]
- [ ]
- [ ]
- [ ]
- [ ]
- [ ]
- [ ]
- [ ]
- [ ]
- [ ]
- [ ]
- [ ]
- [ ]
- [ ]
- [ ]
- [ ]
- [ ]
- [ ]

Organize & Act   *date: __ / __ / ____*

IMPORTANT   NOT IMPORTANT

URGENT

NOT URGENT

*brain*STORM

TASKS

- [ ]
- [ ]
- [ ]
- [ ]
- [ ]
- [ ]
- [ ]
- [ ]
- [ ]
- [ ]

NOTES

Plan & Prep

date: __ / __ / ____

*brain*STORM

TASKS

- ☐
- ☐
- ☐
- ☐
- ☐
- ☐
- ☐
- ☐
- ☐
- ☐

NOTES

Plan & Prep

date: __ / __ / ____

*brain*STORM

TASKS

- [ ]
- [ ]
- [ ]
- [ ]
- [ ]
- [ ]
- [ ]
- [ ]
- [ ]
- [ ]

NOTES

Plan & Prep

date: __ / __ / ____

*brain*STORM

TASKS

Plan & Prep

date: __ / __ / ____

*brain*STORM

TASKS

- ☐
- ☐
- ☐
- ☐
- ☐
- ☐
- ☐
- ☐
- ☐
- ☐

NOTES

Plan & Prep

date: __ / __ / ____

*brain*STORM

TASKS

- [ ]
- [ ]
- [ ]
- [ ]
- [ ]
- [ ]
- [ ]
- [ ]
- [ ]
- [ ]

NOTES

Plan & Prep

date: __ / __ / ____

*brain*STORM

TASKS

- [ ]
- [ ]
- [ ]
- [ ]
- [ ]
- [ ]
- [ ]
- [ ]
- [ ]
- [ ]

NOTES

Plan & Prep

date: __ / __ / ____

*brain*STORM

TASKS

☐ _____
☐ _____
☐ _____
☐ _____
☐ _____
☐ _____
☐ _____
☐ _____
☐ _____
☐ _____

NOTES

_____
_____
_____
_____
_____
_____
_____
_____
_____
_____
_____
_____
_____
_____
_____

Plan & Prep

date: __ / __ / ____

*brain*STORM

TASKS

- [ ]
- [ ]
- [ ]
- [ ]
- [ ]
- [ ]
- [ ]
- [ ]
- [ ]
- [ ]

NOTES

Plan & Prep

date: __ / __ / ____

*brain*STORM

TASKS

- [ ]
- [ ]
- [ ]
- [ ]
- [ ]
- [ ]
- [ ]
- [ ]
- [ ]
- [ ]

NOTES

*brain*STORM

TASKS

☐
☐
☐
☐
☐
☐
☐
☐
☐
☐

NOTES

Plan & Prep

date: __ / __ / ____

*brain*STORM

TASKS

- ☐
- ☐
- ☐
- ☐
- ☐
- ☐
- ☐
- ☐
- ☐
- ☐

NOTES

Plan & Prep

date: __ / __ / ____

*brain*STORM

TASKS

- [ ]
- [ ]
- [ ]
- [ ]
- [ ]
- [ ]
- [ ]
- [ ]
- [ ]
- [ ]

NOTES

Plan & Prep

date: __ / __ / ____

323

*brain*STORM

TASKS

- [ ]
- [ ]
- [ ]
- [ ]
- [ ]
- [ ]
- [ ]
- [ ]
- [ ]
- [ ]

NOTES

Plan & Prep

date: __ / __ / ____

*brain*STORM

TASKS

- [ ]
- [ ]
- [ ]
- [ ]
- [ ]
- [ ]
- [ ]
- [ ]
- [ ]
- [ ]

NOTES

Plan & Prep

date: __ / __ / ____

*brain*STORM

TASKS

- [ ]
- [ ]
- [ ]
- [ ]
- [ ]
- [ ]
- [ ]
- [ ]
- [ ]
- [ ]

NOTES

Plan & Prep

329

*brain*STORM

TASKS

- [ ]
- [ ]
- [ ]
- [ ]
- [ ]
- [ ]
- [ ]
- [ ]
- [ ]
- [ ]

NOTES

Plan & Prep

date: __ / __ / ____

*brain*STORM

TASKS

- ☐ _____
- ☐ _____
- ☐ _____
- ☐ _____
- ☐ _____
- ☐ _____
- ☐ _____
- ☐ _____
- ☐ _____
- ☐ _____

NOTES

Plan & Prep

date: __ / __ / ____

*brain*STORM

TASKS

☐ _____
☐ _____
☐ _____
☐ _____
☐ _____
☐ _____
☐ _____
☐ _____
☐ _____
☐ _____

NOTES

_____
_____
_____
_____
_____
_____
_____
_____
_____
_____
_____
_____
_____
_____
_____

Plan & Prep

date: __ / __ / ____

*brain*STORM

TASKS

- [ ]
- [ ]
- [ ]
- [ ]
- [ ]
- [ ]
- [ ]
- [ ]
- [ ]
- [ ]

NOTES

Plan & Prep

date: __ / __ / ____

*take*NOTE

date: __ / __ / ____

*take*NOTE   *date:* __ / __ / ____

*take*NOTE

date: __ / __ / ____

*take*NOTE

date: __ / __ / ____

*take*NOTE

date: __ / __ / ____

*take*NOTE

date: __ / __ / ____

*take*NOTE   *date:* __ / __ / ____

*take*NOTE

date: __ / __ / ____

*take*NOTE   *date:* __ / __ / ____

*take*NOTE

date: __ / __ / ____

date: __ / __ / ____

*take*NOTE

date: __ / __ / ____

*take*NOTE

*take*NOTE   *date:* __ / __ / ____

*take*NOTE

date: __ / __ / ____

*take*NOTE

*take*NOTE

date: __ / __ / ____

takeNOTE

date: __ / __ / ____

*take*NOTE

date: __ / __ / ____

*take*NOTE

date: __ / __ / ____

*take*NOTE

date: __ / __ / ____

*take*NOTE

date: __ / __ / ____

*take*NOTE

takeNOTE

date: __ / __ / ____

*take*NOTE

date: __ / __ / ____

*take*NOTE

date: __ / __ / ____

*take*NOTE

date: __ / __ / ____

*take*NOTE   *date:* __ / __ / ____

367

index

PAGES   CONTENT

index

index

PAGES   CONTENT

index

PAGES	CONTENT

index

index

PAGES   CONTENT

index

index

PAGES   CONTENT

22146431R00208

Made in the USA
Middletown, DE
14 December 2018